BLOCKBUSTER

How To Build A Million Dollar Tax Business

Even If You Didn't Know How To Prepare a Tax Return

CHAUNCEY HUTTER, JR.

Leading Marketing Consultant & Success Coach to the Tax Industry

Copyright Notice

NO RESELLING OR DUPLICATING THIS BOOK
FOR ANY PURPOSE.

© 2016 RTM, Inc. / All Rights Reserved

ALL RIGHTS ARE RESERVED:

No part of this publication may be reproduced or transmitted in any form or by any means, mechanical or electronic, including photocopying and recording, or by any information storage or retrieval system without permission in writing from the Publisher.

Published under the Copyright Laws of the Library of Congress of the United States of America, by:

RTM, Inc
205 2nd Street S.W.
Charlottesville, VA 22902
www.taxmarketing.com

Disclaimer and/or Legal Notices

While all attempts have been made to verify information provided in this publication, neither the author nor the publisher assumes any responsibility for errors, omissions or contradictory interpretations of the subject matter herein. Any perceived slights of specific people or organizations are unintentional.

This publication is not intended for the use as a source of legal, financial, healthcare or tax advice. The publishers want to stress that the information contained within may be subject to varying state and/or local laws or regulations may apply to the user's particular situation.

The purchaser or reader of this publication assumes responsibility for the use of these materials and information. Adherence to all applicable laws and regulations, both federal and state and local, governing professional licensing, business practices, advertising and all other aspects of doing business in the U.S. or any other jurisdiction is the sole responsibility of the purchaser or reader. RTM, Inc or RTBS assumes no responsibility or liability whatsoever on the behalf of any purchaser or reader of these materials.

Tribute To My Dad

Pop, I wouldn't be the man I am today
if it wasn't for you.

Thank You for the love, mercy and
kindness you've shown me my whole life.

Thank You for saying "YES" when I
first proposed coming to work for your tax
business. I knew nothing about the
industry, but you offered a place
for me to work.

Thank You for allowing me the freedom to make
mistakes (a LOT of them) as I
grew up in business.

And Thank You for being a Godly role model
for me in this world.

Love,
CH, Jr.

RTBS is a marketing consulting and business growth coaching company specializing in helping tax business owners achieve their financial and lifestyle dreams.

Since 1996, thousands of tax professionals throughout North America have participated in RTBS Memberships, Coaching Groups, and Live Training Events and purchased Tax Business Growth Materials.

Chauncey Hutter, Jr, RTBS Founder and President, is best known for his "Renegade" Tax Business Wealth Strategies offered through his Million Dollar Tax Business Builder Success System for tax pros eager to take their tax businesses to the next level.

#   #   #

Schedule permitting, Mr. Hutter charges $10,000 for a day of personal, one-on-one consulting. Other ongoing Coaching Memberships offered by Application Only.

For more information go to:

www.taxmarketing.com

Table of Contents

INTRODUCTION 1

Chapter 1 5
A Starving Crowd
"The Line Was So Long For People To Get Into Our Tax Office, It Stretched Out The Door, Down The Street And Around The Block.... Literally!"

Chapter 2 17
A "Real World" Back Story: Foundational Strategies For Building A Tax Biz Empire

Chapter 3 31
Little-Known Tax Biz Success Secrets Simplified

Chapter 4 51
Top 10 Best Questions To Ask (Then Answer) For Your Tax Biz

Chapter 5 67
Advanced Tax Biz Marketing

Chapter 6 81
"Work Less ... Make More" Tax Biz Profit Strategies

Chapter 7 99
Increasing Your Tax Biz's #1 Source for New Clients

Chapter 8 117
Tax Biz Wealth Is In THE PROCESS

Chapter 9 131
Effective Tax Biz Leadership Dramatically
Reduces Your Stress & Headaches

Chapter 10 149
The Tax Biz Millionaire Mindset

Chapter 11 161
Finally! ...How to Achieve Your Tax Biz
Dreams

Chapter 12 177
For Tax Biz Owners: The Opportunity
of Our Lifetime

Final Thoughts .... In The Land Of
The Blind, The One Eyed Man Is King 183

Chauncey's Recommended Tax Business
Success RESOURCES 189

What Other Tax Business Owners Are Saying ....

*"With ONE IDEA I got from Chauncey, I came away with a **new strategy that puts $45,000 in my pocket EVERY YEAR** at no extra cost to me."*

Jon Neal, CPA, MST, PFS
The Neal Group

*"Chauncey helped turn my office systems completely around ... he guided me on how to hire and train some great preparers ...**now I work LESS HOURS and make MORE MONEY** ... plus our tax returns are processed faster so our clients love the changes!"*

Karen Spencer -- Accountability Tax Services

*"I was struggling to stay afloat ... **but with Chauncey's marketing I doubled my clients** ... I can say without a doubt, I would not be in the tax business today if not for Chauncey's tremendous guidance and promotional strategies."*

Ed Bove, Tax Express

*"Chauncey's experience with 20+ tax offices has been invaluable ... **PRICELESS!**"*

Brian Roark, CPA
Integrity Tax Group

AN AMAZING TRUE LIFE STORY

How A Son Takes Over His Father's $50,000 A Year Tax Preparation Business, Builds A Multi-Million Dollar Company ... Even Causing Several National Tax Franchise Offices to Shut Down in the Process!

And how that same fellow has since helped over 3,350 tax practitioners, electronic filers, EA's, CPA's and other tax business owners dramatically, quickly increase their earnings with his methods -- *even though most of them were skeptics to start with.*

Let me introduce myself. My name is Chauncey Hutter, Jr.

And did you know -- **I can't even prepare my own tax return!** *(Or, anybody else's for that matter.)*

But that didn't stop me from growing a small, two-room tax office with a couple of part-time employees into a multi-MILLION dollar business in 15 different market areas (w/ 24 locations) and employing over 400 people during the peak of tax season while generating over $4 Million Dollars in tax preparation and electronic filing sales during the first 100 days of each year!

So how does a guy with NO tax experience come into a small tax office and build a MILLION dollar tax preparation business in just a few short tax seasons?

Well, that's a "secret" I've kept to myself.

Until now.

BLOCKBUSTER
How To Build A Million Dollar Tax Business

You see, there are MANY little-known tax business development strategies I've discovered that make growing a tax business to the MILLION dollar level much easier and faster. (I just wish somebody would have given me a BOOK LIKE THIS when I first started.) Back in the day, it would have made my life a whole heck of a lot easier!

One of the SECRETS most tax professionals DON'T realize is Even The Most Tax Law-Knowledgeable, Highest Paid, Credentialed Professional And The Hardest Working Tax Business Owner On The Planet Will Live With An Average (Or Even Below Average), Disappointing Income Without A Consistent, Steady Flow Of New Clients Coming Into Their Tax Office!

If you think that since you are a tax professional, everyone in town who needs tax help is going to beat your door down looking to give YOU their money because you've got the most tax experience or you've gone to more tax seminars this year or you have some extra letters behind your name etc. -- you're just not living in reality!

It's called *"dream-ville"* ... when you think increasing your tax skills automatically translates into being able to stuff more money in your pockets at the end of each day. (If that were true, our tax business would be dead broke because I still don't know how to fill out a 1040 EZ!)

The point is:
BEING GOOD AT WHAT YOU DO
IS NOT GOOD ENOUGH!

I cannot be gentle about this, even though I know you won't like hearing it: this is the fundamental truth that can liberate you from laboring mightily for your dollars, settling for an "average" income and can empower you to truly TRANSFORM your tax practice into a very different, super-high-income business that'll make your peers and competitors absolutely green with envy.

<u>Here it is:</u>

Continuing to believe that your expertise and knowledge entitles you to success ..... resenting those "big guys" who use mass advertising ..... trying to increase your income by increasing your knowledge of tax law ..... these are all losing strategies in today's competitive marketplace.

There is a different, much more productive way to THINK about your business. And once you mentally accept it's OK to be different than your competition, you'll be on your way to growing your tax practice to the next level of success!

Now, if you are ready to hear it ... I'm ready to "spill the beans" about Real Tax Business Success!

Turn to Chapter 1 and let's take a look .....

Chapter 1

A Starving Crowd

"The Line Was So Long For People To Get Into Our Tax Office, It Stretched Out The Door, Down The Street And Around The Block.... Literally!"

Imagine walking up and seeing a line of people standing outside the door of your tax office—a line running down the steps, winding down the sidewalk, stretching out across the road through the parking lot, onto the sidewalk on the other side of the street, down that road and around "The Block." Literally: A very long line of people wanting to come into your tax office instead of the brand name competition across the street. These clients are eager to do business with you, NOT your competition. And when they get inside, you are going to get paid (on the higher end of the fee scale) for helping them file their taxes. Picture this scenario for you and your tax business in the future.

I don't have to imagine this picture. What I'm about to tell you is a true story that really happened in our tax business. We experienced a "starving crowd."

So let me explain the starving crowd concept for you. I didn't invent this concept. It came from Gary Halbert, who, back when he was alive, was the leading sales copywriter of his era. He famously stated, "In business, if you could give me any advantage, I'll take a starving crowd every time." The example he used was, "Look, if you and I both owned a hamburger stand, and we were in a contest to see who could sell the most hamburgers, what advantage would you like to have on your side to help you win?" Then he would ask people and they'd say, "Well, I want a special sauce," or "I want superior meat," or "I want sesame seed buns." Of course, others would say, "Give me a great location, location, location." Others said, "I just want the best price."

And Gary said, "No, I'm going to beat you all, no matter what you have, if I have access to a starving crowd. I will win every time." It makes sense because if somebody is just desperate to get what you're offering, it doesn't matter how good you are. Now I'm not saying you don't have to be good at preparing taxes, because you do want to be great at what you do.

However, **a starving crowd makes everything you do much easier. A starving crowd enables you to make sales at will – even if you have very average marketing or promotional ads.**

Now, this happened to us back in the early days of electronic filing. There was a new, faster tax return—refund anticipation loans were available then—and tax business owners who were early adopters grew like crazy. They increased their client base; some say it was like shooting fish in a barrel. I'll just say it this way: It was not hard to grow your tax business. For tax business owners who entered the electronic tax filing game early, we were just slammed with new clients—mainly because we were giving the starving crowd what they wanted. And at the time, the main service they craved was quick money in the form of those really fast refund loan checks from the late 1980s and early 1990s.

Packed In Like Sardines

In my first tax season working for my father's tax business, the room was wall-to-wall with people. It was like a rock concert with everyone trying to move up front to the stage. We don't have a small tax office. But there were so many people trying to get in the door to be served, I had to stand up on a chair with a clipboard, raise my voice pretty loud (but not yelling because I didn't want to freak people out) and say, "Look, if your name is not on this sign-in sheet, you're not going to get service today." I said it in a nice, but authoritative tone. I wanted to be clear: "We can't handle everybody in this office, so you've got to write your name here, and get in line, because we're about to lock the door."

Now, it pains me even today to write these words. But we did have to shut that door at five o'clock that day (and turn away many more new clients) simply because we could not handle the amount of people coming in our office. We'd already serviced a long list of clients that day, but we only had so many computers and so many employees.

This is a great problem to have, right?

Six Months Earlier

OK, let's go back six months, in August, before tax season. I had just come to work for my dad. I was "green" and very inexperienced to say the least. I didn't know anything about taxes. Naturally, what was the first thing my dad wanted me to do when I came to work for his tax business? Of course, he wanted me to go take an income tax school class at one of the brand-name tax firms. Now this brand-name was a national franchise—starts with a "b" and rhymes with "clock."

BLOCKBUSTER
How To Build A Million Dollar Tax Business

I went to the tax class to honor my dad's wishes, but I knew this was not what I needed to do with my time. I hated taxes. I knew that learning how to file a tax return was not the way I could help our family's tax business grow. So I went to a few tax classes and learned a little bit for a couple of weeks – but couldn't stand it. Then I decided to made friends with some of the smartest people in the class because I wanted to hire them before tax season to come work for us. I dropped out because I knew I was a marketer, a salesperson, someone that drums up business—not someone who sits behind a desk and does tax returns. That's just not how I'm wired.

What's funny is I had been laid off earlier in July. I worked for a hardware company that sold windows and doors to construction businesses. The company was not doing well, and so they called all the employees into a meeting one day and said, "We're closing our doors. You've got three weeks to finish whatever outstanding issues you have with your contractors."

I finished up that job and began looking for other work-related opportunities. Within a week, I contacted a friend of mine who was the associate pastor at our church. He happened to have been a guidance counselor before going to seminary to become a minister. I sat with him for about an hour explaining my situation to him. At the end, he said, "I really think you ought to go work for your dad," to which I quickly countered, "No, he's in the tax business, and I know nothing about taxes. Let's talk about something different."

Well, we spent some more time together hashing through various scenarios and at the end of it, my pastor friend boldly exclaimed, "I REALLY think you should consider going to work for your father. You can spend your time drumming up business, and your dad can offer tax-related services to clients. I truly feel like you would make a great team."

BLOCKBUSTER
How To Build A Million Dollar Tax Business

First Day Working In The Tax Industry

Obviously, I took his advice, and now I was working for my dad. It was a hot summer day in August. I literally didn't know anything about the tax industry! But I didn't care. I just walked out the door, walked across the street and down the road to the first business I saw. It was a shoe repair business. I walked in, introduced myself and explained that I worked at the tax business right up the road (I pointed because it probably wasn't 50 or 75 yards away) and I just blurted out, "Do you need help with your taxes?" (Pretty original opening line, huh?) Then, he looked at me and said, "Actually, I do."

I didn't realize how funny this was until later, but he headed to a side room and came back out with a couple shoe boxes of receipts and tax-related papers. As it turns out, he hadn't filed his taxes in a couple years. I didn't know the whole shoebox joke until later on, when tax season came. On April 14th and 15th we'd get dozens of procrastinators coming in our tax office with shoeboxes full of receipts. Since you're in the tax business, you know exactly what I'm talking about. But I was a newbie, and I didn't know anything. So the business owner gave me these shoeboxes, and since he is in a shoe repair business, he had lots of them!

Then I followed up and said, "Look, I appreciate you giving me all this tax information, but I need to get some type of deposit from you BEFORE we start doing any work." I just instinctively knew I needed to get paid something to solidify this sale. And so, he wrote me a check for a hundred bucks to start, and then fifteen minutes later, I walked back into my dad's office, and I said, "Okay, Dad, here's the first sale! Here's a hundred bucks to start, and here's a couple shoeboxes full of receipts. I just made a sale right across the street over there."

He couldn't believe it. "Really?" he said. "You just left! You weren't gone fifteen minutes!" I just smiled and said, "This is how I roll!" We laughed because it was fun making my first sale fifteen minutes on the job.

BUT HERE IS AN IMPORTANT POINT:

I just got started. I got in motion. I took action towards a goal of increasing sales.

I used good ol' fashion shoe leather and walked out the tax office door and began searching for new business. Truth was, I didn't know anything else to do.

Many tax professionals are struggling. They are dying on the vine with little-to-no new clients coming in their door. However, they've never just walked out their door, gone to the closest neighboring businesses and introduced themselves either. Just walk in with a simple gift—drop it off and ask if you could serve their small business in anyway related to taxes and financial matters.

That must be a terrifying thought to many tax professionals because most have NEVER actually done it. But if you're a tax pro, it's really not that big a deal to ask if someone needs tax help. I wasn't even a tax professional. I was just a guy out there asking if we could help somebody in the area of taxes.

"WHO'S THIS GUY NAMED ... FICA?"

My first introduction to taxes was when I was sixteen years old and I was working as a lifeguard at the pool where our family went in the summer. I think I was probably making three dollars an hour. I worked twenty hours that first week so I

BLOCKBUSTER
How To Build A Million Dollar Tax Business

was looking forward to getting my first paycheck. I could do the math: twenty hours times three bucks. I was going to get paid sixty dollars. The paychecks came and I opened up the envelope to see my sixty dollar check. It was only for fifty-two dollars? I thought, "What happened here? Somebody took my money!"

I went home to my dad, and I showed him the check, and I said, "Dad! Who's FICA? FICA's got some of this money!" He laughed SO hard. My dad said, "Hold on a second." And he called in my mom from the kitchen, still laughing, "Honey, honey, come here. Okay, Chauncey say that again. Ask me that same question again ... listen to this."

And I said, "Well, I just wanted to know who FICA is. He has some of my money. Just look at my paycheck." And they both busted out in laughter. Then my dad proclaimed, "Welcome to the real world, son. It's called death and taxes." Then he proceeded to give me that whole speech ... and that was my first introduction to Uncle Sam.

My First Tax Season

Now, fast forward to actually working in a tax business. My younger brother took a little break from school and decided to work for my dad as a bookkeeper. He was self-taught, and a really smart guy. I would go out on sales calls and my brother would stay back in the office and handle the taxes, bookkeeping and payroll.

When we got to tax season, I didn't realize what was about to happen. It was January, and I wasn't doing tax returns. I was outside the office beating the bushes for new clients. I was going to nearby convenience stores, high traffic grocery stores and other area businesses to see if they would help us get the word out about our tax business. I was doing all the guerilla marketing, grass- roots-style and word-on-the-streets type of promotions you can think of. I was not doing a lot of fancy, paid marketing and advertising. It was all grunt work at this point. That was what I knew to do at the time. Just beat a bunch of bushes, and see how many new clients fall out.

When I wasn't out trying to drum up new business, I played receptionist. I was answering the phone and talking to the people when they walked in. I asked a ton of questions. How had they heard about us? What services were they most interested in? And why? (This was key to know so we could market to them in the future.) I did the same thing on the phone with existing clients and prospects calling in.

Then, intuitively, I thought I better begin tracking these answers. I started with a pencil and a piece of paper. (When in doubt, use what you've got at the time.) When I tallied up my notes at the end of each day, I noticed a pattern. I saw that out of every ten calls that were coming in, nine of them were new. New people who had never been with us. And I'm thinking to myself, "The writing's on the wall. We're about to get slammed!"

Preparing For A Tidal Wave

As the first few weeks of tax season passed, we grew increasingly busy. We had to hire more people to help prepare tax returns. My dad and brother would train them. Plus, there were existing part-time people who decided to work longer hours. We grew busier and busier. I remember going into a computer store on a Thursday evening and doubling our computer capacity overnight. We hired additional people and trained them on the fly. This is what a starving crowd cramming into your tax office will do. We could barely get the work done. But again, this is a nice problem to have!

BLOCKBUSTER
How To Build A Million Dollar Tax Business

The stream of new clients was so great that we had to go to a drop-off system and a third shift. That meant some of our employees worked into the night and through the early morning. A small group would come in about four o'clock in the afternoon and they'd work all night until about two or three o'clock in the morning, or whenever the work for the day was completed. Then we had a few of the part-time employees (our "early birds") who came into the office around five or six o'clock in the morning before they would go to their regular jobs during the day. These folks would check the work from the night before, electronically transmit whatever was needed, print out refund checks, fix and resend the rejected returns and just do whatever was needed to start the new day off right. Then our regular staff would begin taking clients for that day at eight thirty or nine o'clock each morning.

(Yes, we almost had an around-the-clock work day during the peak of tax season.)

Our Competition's Response To
The Starving Crowd

We did whatever we had to do to give the starving crowd what they wanted. What was our competition doing? We had competing tax businesses all around our tax office. What were those tax business owners doing about the starving crowd in our city? Well, the national tax franchises and other independent tax firms chose not to hire and train any new employees. They kept the same amount of computer equipment they'd had the previous year. They decided to keep the same system for serving clients they always had.

Bottom Line: They didn't change a thing.

Did these other tax firms get tons of inquiries about their services, too? Of course. The feeding frenzy was on. But they chose NOT to update their tax season office processes to handle the influx of new prospects seeking out their tax services. Consequently, the brand name competition's turn-around time for helping their tax clients was approximately four or five DAYS. In our office, we changed everything we could to streamline our processes for a 12-to-36 HOUR turn-around time! Speed is what the starving crowd wanted ... so that's what we gave them.

The word of mouth on the street was spreading like wild fire. **Giving the starving crowd what they want is extremely helpful for referrals.** Word on the street was travelling through work places and neighborhoods and wherever people gathered in the community. And of course, there were a number of folks who had their taxes prepared and filed at other tax firms. So by the time they found out about us, they couldn't do anything different until next year. We got a bunch of phone calls, too, saying, "I just wanted to call and make sure what my friend said was true about what you guys are doing. I'm coming to you next year!" We found out some of the best marketing for next tax season came from taking care of clients this tax season.

What About Today's Starving Crowd?

I've started by giving you a real-life example from back when I first entered the tax industry. But let's talk about now. What is today's starving crowd?

As of this writing, there is a little thing called Obamacare. For us in the tax industry, we know it as The Affordable Care Act. We're in the early stages. **A starving crowd is being birthed from the healthcare industry injecting itself into the tax industry.** There are some early adopters now. Tax

BLOCKBUSTER
How To Build A Million Dollar Tax Business

business owners who have decided to position themselves as the first movers are gaining expert status over their peers in whatever city they are in. Obamacare is not going away. So the Affordable Care Act will have a significant impact on the tax industry for many years to come.

Another starving crowd and one of the fastest growing markets in our country, is the Latino population. For some tax business owners, this is not new information. About twenty years ago, our tax business opened separate offices to properly service this clientele. We would hire Spanish-speaking employees to help us not only prepare the tax returns efficiently, but also to get the word out about our services. Even today, you see many national tax franchises making significant moves to cater to this fast growing market.

But even if you prefer NOT to target either of these first two starving crowd examples, there are other options in your market area. Just find the underserved people groups who live and work around you. One way to find these new prospects is by occupation. There are always regular, hard-working people who have had bad experiences when it comes to filing their taxes.

As a tax professional, you know the common mistakes most taxpayers make when they try to prepare their taxes themselves. If you take some time to survey your own clients, you'll find some commonalities within your list. And since birds of a feather flock together, you can locate the underserved markets and tap into taxpayers "hungry" for your tax services. Depending on your area, there could be dozens and dozens of small niche markets acting like mini starving crowds. And you just need to tap into them.

BLOCKBUSTER
How To Build A Million Dollar Tax Business

My main point for you in this opening chapter:

Find a starving crowd and take care of them better than any other tax business owner in your area.

Starving crowds make exceptionally good pavers on the roads leading to million-dollar tax businesses. I can speak from experience on this.

And if your tax business gets this first piece of the puzzle right, you'll have a head start over your competition and will be well on your way to taking your tax business to the next level.

Chapter 2

A "Real World" Back Story: Foundational Strategies For Building A Tax Biz Empire

I'm going to share my Foundational Strategies for Building a Tax Business Empire. To do this, I'll pull back the curtain and reveal a handful of little-known stories very few people have heard me share. These real-world back stories are not only instructive, but offer practical insight on how best to operate and grow your tax business.

You'll discover how to build an organization with a significantly high level of success, including massive profits, thousands of clients, as many quality employees as you need and much less stress, anxiety and headaches than you ever thought possible. Yes, there are different types of problems when your tax business reaches higher levels of success. But in many ways, these "issues" are much easier to deal with once your tax business is running on autopilot. In my view, the harder part comes in the early days when you are just scratching and clawing, trying to figure out how to maximize your success. Hopefully my back stories will help cut your learning curve significantly so the process for growing a million-dollar tax business becomes much easier for you!

BLOCKBUSTER
How To Build A Million Dollar Tax Business

My Dad Starts A Bookkeeping & Tax Business

I remember that when I was a kid, my dad did "bookkeeping and taxes" (at least that's what he told me when I had to give my elementary school teacher an answer to draw a picture of my father's occupation). I grew up in a tax business family. My dad chose to get into the tax business and start selling bookkeeping accounts when I was only a year old.

Some business opportunity guy came along one day and said, "Hey, you'd be better off selling these write-up systems that help small businesses track their revenue and expenses each month. If you could sell a couple of these a week, you'd be making more money than you are at your current job." And like many entrepreneurs, my dad said, "I'm going to go for it. I'll walk away from a steady paycheck and try to increase my income and not put a limit on my earning potential."

My dad gave notice and left his job. He set a goal of a hundred clients that first year, or two sales a week. Sure enough, a year later, my dad reached his goal, plus a few additional clients. And then tax season came around and all these small business owners inquired, "Well, who's going do my tax return?" So my dad got into the tax preparation business pretty quickly.

However, from the beginning my dad knew that he did NOT want to do the work of preparing the tax returns. So he went out and hired a part-time employee. My dad did SOME of the tax prep work, but he knew that he needed to stick to his core activity of selling and growing his business. **It was important to my dad, in this foundational time of expanding his bookkeeping and tax practice, that he hire other employees to do the manual**

labor tasks of servicing the accountants. My dad knew that if he did all the "work" he just sold, he would never have time to develop and grow the business.

My dad HAD the time and COULD have "saved some money" by not hiring a staff person.

But his TIME INVESTMENT in selling and growing the business [a much higher payoff compared to a smaller dollar-per-hour bookkeeping or tax prep task] was more important. This was wisdom in the early stages of his tax business.

A Family Man DURING Tax Season

As I grew older, I remember my dad coming home between four and four-thirty every afternoon during tax season. Now, you're thinking to yourself, "How in the world is this guy who's growing his tax business leaving his office before five o'clock during tax season?" **Even though my dad was very busy during tax season, he CHOSE to come home early to see his kids.** (By the way, this has had a huge positive impact on me as a dad during tax season.) He wanted to be around his family.

Back then, I remember, the local newspaper was delivered in the afternoons instead of the mornings. So the newspaper delivery boy would show up right about four o'clock and that's when my dad would sit down and read the paper. My little brother and sister and I were taught to wait and give my dad fifteen minutes read the news of the day. I remember we'd take off his shoes for him and just sit on the floor in the living room waiting for him to turn the last page of the paper. Of course, in dramatic fashion, he'd toss the newspaper off to the side and jump down on the floor to wrestle with us. We'd play, go outside and run around, swing on the swing set, throw a ball and have fun.

At dinner, he'd spend time with my mom. She'd tuck us in at bedtime. Then my mom and dad had about an hour together before he'd go to bed about eight-thirty or nine o'clock. Then the next day would come and my dad was up early and working in the office by five or six o'clock in the morning. This way, he could get a full day of work in and be back at our house again around four o'clock.

Here's my point: **My dad prioritized his schedule, even in the busiest season, by what he valued most.** <u>He valued his wife and his children most. Again, he was a great role model for me.</u>

I've spent many years as a marketing consultant and a success coach in the tax industry, and I talk to a lot of different tax pros about their problems and how to resolve some of their most painful issues. And I'll tell you the truth. Many tax business owners will confide in me that they do a pretty good job in this area for eight or nine months of the year. But the two or three months of the year during tax season, where they're at their wit's end, pulling their hair out, THEY ADMIT THIS HAS BEEN A PROBLEM FOR THEM FOR YEARS.

When you're building a foundation to grow a tax business to a significantly higher level, that's great. Even if your tax practice is very small right now – that's ok. **You STILL have to prioritize your schedule (even in your busiest season) and give time to what you value most.** <u>Committing to this Foundational Base is very important to do NOW.</u>

I Was An Average Student, My Usual Grades Were C's

When I was in high school, I had an English teacher who didn't like me that much. I was a cut-up in class, and I was making C's in her classroom. So I wasn't the best student in her class, but I did want to go to a university after I graduated my senior year. So one day, I was very serious in her class. I went up to her desk and I said, "Ms. Burgess, I want to go to college. Would you write me a letter of recommendation?" She turned around, looked at me, and just laughed out loud in front of all the students. And then she just blurted out, "Chauncey, you've got to be kidding me. You are not college material. You should think about going into the army. You should not go to college."

Well, I was taken aback by her statement. I had it in my mind that I wanted to go to college. No one had ever told me I couldn't go to college. I might not have straight A's, but I thought I could go to college somewhere. Well, it's one thing to yell at a student for cutting up in class. But it's a whole different thing to completely squash a young student's idea of what he wants to do in the next phase of life.

So when my mom heard this, she went completely ballistic. She just couldn't believe that a teacher would say that to a student so obnoxiously and in front of the whole class. My mom came to school the next day and had a heated conversation with the principal. (I'm sure Ms. Burgess got an ear full, too.)

Ultimately, I didn't listen to the negative voice of my teacher. I went on to graduate from Appalachian State University. :--)

You will have people in your life (even today) that will discourage you. They will "poo-poo" your dreams or whatever you're actively pursuing in the next phase of your life. If it's growing your tax business, they'll say, "No, you could never make a million dollars in your tax business." DO NOT LISTEN TO THIS VOICE.

People will go out of their way to discourage you from moving forward in your life. Others will comment, "Yeah, that's probably not for you. You shouldn't do that. You'll probably fail."

This type of negative talk is extremely destructive! Do not listen to these people.

Get them out of your life. Number one, if you're going to grow your tax business to the next level, you cannot have those kinds of people talking in your ears.

That means you don't let the people who are hateful, the folks who are downers, the glass-half-empty types -- you don't let those folks cause you to doubt yourself.

Don't allow negative people to speak into your life about your dreams. But if they live under the same roof, it's time (now) to grow some thick skin. **Every successful million-dollar tax business builder I know has learned to grow thick skin.**

"Winning" Business Lesson I Learn From My First Marketing Professor

People ask me all the time, "How did you get in to be a marketing consultant?" Well, when I was younger, I didn't even know what marketing was. I went to college, and in my second year (spring semester), somebody came up to me and said, "You have to declare a major." I said, "A major? What do you mean by major?" And he answered, "You have to declare a study to focus on." I thought, "Well, I don't know what that would be." The guy saw my puzzled look and said, "You've got to pick something; today's the deadline." So I said, "Okay, give me the list of majors I'm supposed to pick from." I'm thinking, "I like business, but there's so many different business majors on these pages."

BLOCKBUSTER
How To Build A Million Dollar Tax Business

So I literally closed my eyes and flipped open the booklet in the business section listing all of the majors, and just put my finger down on a spot on the page. I opened my eyes and looked, and my finger was on something called marketing. That's how I picked my college major. I majored in marketing.

[And just for the record, the story I'm about to tell you is the only thing practical that I learned and could use after graduation. Everything else university professors teach on marketing is all theory and textbook stuff. Nothing you can use in the real world to actually grow a business and make any money.]

So I went to my first marketing class and I loved it. I thought, "Hey, I did a great job picking my major!" Then the following semester, I attended the higher level marketing class. On the first day of class, the professor stood up and declared, "Okay, here's how we're going to grade this class: There'll be only one A, and the rest will have lower grades."

For the smart people, this was a big problem. If someone got a 95 and another student earned a 98, only the higher grade made the A. Several students complained, but the professor barked back, "I don't grade like everyone else -- my grading system is based on the real world. In this context, the real world is this class. So I will grade my class just like the real world does. There's only one person who wins – the person who makes the sale or who gets the deal – everybody else gets less."

Well, I was fascinated by this because I'm a big competitor. I looked around the room and thought to myself, "This sounds good to me." Now, just to fast forward, I didn't make the A, but I made a good grade (B+) because I worked hard and enjoyed it.

That professor taught me a very valuable lesson which I remember and use to this day:

BLOCKBUSTER
How To Build A Million Dollar Tax Business

There's only one winner in the real world ... and second place does not get paid.

And that's what I mean by winner or loser. If you're trying to make a sale in the tax business, you have prospects calling your office, trying to figure out what tax business they're going to use to file their taxes with Uncle Sam. You are competing with every other tax business they see on their local Google search.

Historically, tax businesses are horrific at doing any kind of quality salesmanship over the phone. Your tax office could be average at converting a phone inquiry into an in-person meeting in your office. **But as long as you are better than your competition, you win! You get the A! You make the sale, which means YOU get paid!**

When you're running a tax practice, getting a sale and getting paid is what keeps you in business. If you don't make the sale and don't get paid, you'll go out of business pretty quickly. The point is, my professor in this particular marketing class, really helped shape my mindset to focus on winning. And winning for a business owner is making the sale!

Selling Door-To-Door Gave Me A Million Dollar Education!

I graduated from college. None of the companies I interviewed with my senior year offered me a job. So I went back to my hometown of Charlottesville, VA and took my first job as a door-to-door sales guy. (I sold Water Conditioning Equipment for Culligan.)

Being a door-to-door salesman actually taught me a million-dollar lesson. (I mean this in literal terms.) What I learned from that experience was instrumental in helping our tax business gain over 27,000 new tax clients from my marketing campaigns.

Okay, now I was a college graduate knocking on doors to sell stuff. (By the way, I was completely fine with this. You gotta eat somehow.) I would pull into a driveway, go up to a house and knock on the door; and guess what would happen when someone opened it? The person standing in the doorway would see I was selling something, and they would shut the door in my face ASAP.

<u>Note:</u> If you go knock on enough doors and have this same "facial" experience, you'll find out really quick that you can't just keep doing the same thing over and over again and expect the door not to get shut in your face. You have to try something different. (Unless, of course, you don't want to sell anything.) Since I was paid on commission, I actually DID want to make a sale!

By the way, guess how much time I had between the door opening and shutting? About three seconds. When I was knocking on doors, I had to come up with a line, a phrase, something to buy me another ten or twenty seconds. Then if the door was still open, I needed another line or two to persuade them to give me another minute.

If you haven't made the connection yet, **THIS IS EXACTLY WHAT HAPPENS WHEN YOU PROMOTE YOUR TAX BUSINESS.** <u>You spend money on an ad, a marketing campaign, a new sales letter, your website, any promotional piece – no matter what it is, you've got to grab attention.</u>

In your ad, the first line buys you time for the second line, the first paragraph buys you time for the second paragraph, and on and on and on. That's what salesmanship in print is all about. (The same thing applies to non-print broadcast media.)

I learned this from being a door-to-door salesman because you're never going to make a sale if you don't grab their attention and entice them into reading, or listening, or watching, or whatever. You have to stop them in their tracks and cause them to pay attention to you, or they will never call your tax office, email you, or go to your website.

I've never forgotten this Million Dollar Lesson.

Foundational Tax Business Success Lessons Learned

Here are a few more foundational lessons I learned:

It is vital you don't try and grow your tax business alone. Hire other quality employees to work IN your tax practice. You invest most of your time working ON your business.

And remember, get crystal clear about your home and work boundaries. This is more than a time management issue. It's a self-governance issue for the success of your overall life. Determine what's most important in your life. Dictate your agenda. Don't let circumstances dictate you and control your life.

Next, did you know there are a lot of really smart people who get caught up in the fear of making mistakes, or just failure in general? There's a lot of perfectionism in the tax industry and that approach is not conducive for growing a million-dollar tax business.

If you want to be successful, then you'll have to always be moving forward quickly. Decisive will be your middle name. A sense of urgency to beat your competition will always be in your mind.

Now, I'm not saying that if you're a perfectionist or you're really smart, you can't do what I'm talking about. **I am saying you can be a C student just like me AND be street smart AND do just what you have to do to be successful.** I didn't care about trying to avoid mistakes. I'm not interested in making mistakes, but I'm not afraid to make them either because I learn from them!

I also decided to grow some thick skin because so many people kept telling me how I was doing things completely different from everyone else in the tax industry. (They were implying I was doing everything wrong in a nice way.)

<u>Note: Doing the opposite of everyone else in the tax industry is an excellent strategy because that means you're probably doing a bunch of stuff right. If you're doing the opposite of the masses, you're probably in good shape.</u>

Okay, back to thickening your skin. Don't let other people dictate what you should or shouldn't do. You do what you think is best. Now if you're following me and my tax business success material, you'll be going against the grain big time. I have a renegade approach that helps you stand out and enables you to magnetically attract more well-matched tax clients, versus them going to your competition.

Of course, having laser-like focus on what's most important for your business is key. In my mind, that's making the sale. Let's be frank about this. **If you don't make the sale, nothing else matters! Nothing happens in your business until a sale is made.** You could have the highest quality service, all the fancy degrees and even professional licenses, but if the phone's not ringing, if the emails aren't coming in, if no one's walking through your door ... the letters on the back of your name just don't matter that much.

Success starts with making the sale.

Before we finish this chapter, I just wanted to emphasize the marketing side of success.

Marketing is first.

It's actually the first thing before the sale. **Marketing is finding out who is interested in your tax services and pre-framing your expert positioning.** Even before they call you on the phone, they should have a feel for who you are and what you do because of the marketing you've already released.

Salesmanship is what you say to a prospect when they call or come into your office, depending on their wants, needs and desires; then close the sale. (That's salesmanship.) But the key to getting the sale is getting the marketing right first!

Lastly, I just want to paint a picture for you about leading your tax business.

Be an orchestra leader.

What I mean is, oversee your business. Make your business better by showing others how to do what you have done, and pour into them and make them better. Don't be the tuba player in the orchestra. You need to stop playing the music. It gets exhausting having to hold up the heavy instruments. But since you are the owner, you could switch around and play some other instruments, too – right? You are good enough to perform multiple tasks in your tax office. But the problem is, you're still playing an instrument. (Hint: You're still working IN your business, not working ON your business by orchestrating everyone else's work.)

You could also get too involved in helping everyone else "play their instruments" in your tax office. (This is NOT what a successful orchestra leader's role looks like.) By getting too involved, your employees can't play their instruments correctly. If they have to stop and run everything through you, your "help" (too controlling) is actually hurting the overall orchestra. The same thing happens way too often in tax offices. Employees have to "run it through you" (the owner) and as a result, your tax business doesn't flow well. The truth is, in this operational model, you don't have the time or space to grow because the owner is too involved in the daily tasks. In this scenario, <u>YOU ARE THE BOTTLENECK</u>.

You're down in the weeds, trying to be the savior of everyone else's tax problems, which guarantees a ceiling over your head.

I promise you can't grow your tax business to the multi-million dollar level if that ceiling stays right above you.

Do you remember the guy from Wendy's, Dave Thomas?

I heard him speak one time and he had a great story about working back in the kitchen, making hamburgers, in the early days. He said, "Nobody made a better hamburger than me." He made the best hamburgers. But he also knew that if he was the only one in the kitchen making hamburgers, he would never reach his dream of building a large fast-food restaurant chain.

He knew he had to delegate the making of the "core product" of his business. Dave Thomas chose NOT to have the perfect hamburger. On a scale of 1-10, when he made his burger, it was a 10. But he had to train somebody else that could make a burger on a scale of at least 8 or 9 out of 10 – every time. Dave openly acknowledged that when someone else beside him made a hamburger, it wasn't going to be as good as his burger. (The key was – it would be GOOD ENOUGH.) It would be a quality hamburger.

In Wendy's case, in order for Dave Thomas to live his dream of building a fast-food empire, he needed to get out of the kitchen.

Now, let me say this as nicely as I know how. **You cannot grow your tax business to the million-dollar level if you're the person "flipping the burgers."**

During tax season, is most of your time spent preparing taxes? I'm not saying don't ever do tax returns, but I am saying, "You can't be in the kitchen flipping the burgers MOST of the time."

You can (should) prepare some tax returns – sometimes. (We'll get into what and how to delegate later in this book.) But for now, know this:

There are PLENTY of other things you can do with your time to keep your tax business on the million dollar road to success.

That's what the rest of this book is all about.

<u>Chapter 3</u>

Little-Known Tax Biz Success Secrets Simplified

I just want to give a little disclaimer before we get into this.

First of all, I'm a marketing consultant. I've been providing marketing consulting services for tax business owners for many years. During this time, I've made a couple of observations when discussing the subject of secrets. The real world truth about secrets is that some people will know some of the things I'm about to talk about, while others won't have a clue.

But there's a **very important distinction between "knowing" and "doing."**

Ask yourself this: Are you depositing large sums of money into your bank account because you are DOING something most others don't know about? Or, can you only say, "Yeah, I know about that secret."

There's also a BIG difference between doing something and doing it the right way. In ninety-nine percent of what I'm about to reveal, tax pros either don't know the strategy or they do know yet are NOT executing "the secret" properly in order to maximize success and grow their tax business to the next level.

What I mean is this: Keep an open mind. You may have heard of some of the material in this chapter. Maybe you used to know a strategy but haven't used it to make money in a very long time. (By the way, in the real world – this counts. The teller at your bank isn't going to say no to your deposit just because you earned this money from remembering something you used to do years ago.)

Or maybe a particular secret is right there on your to-do list. But having a new savvy tax business-building technique on your to-do list (or again, knowing it in your head) is completely different from actually saying, "Yes, I'm making six figures in my tax business because I'm doing X, Y and Z on that particular strategy."

We are talking about two completely different worlds here. **And my whole goal of this chapter is to get you from "knowing in your head" to "following a systematic process" for adding wealth to your tax practice.**

Don't be the "Oh, I know that" guy. Instead, show me where you're put a success secret into action. Show me the implementation steps. Show me the money in the bank from where this strategy improved your tax business.

Let's be doers of these secrets, not just the hearers and the think-about-it people. Don't just put these success techniques on your to-do list to die a slow death, never actually getting them done or executed successfully in your office. Bottom line: **I want to encourage you to commit to making a difference in your tax business by implementing what I'm talking about -- not just thinking about it, but actually doing it.** I promise you will experience a significant boost in your business.

The Three M's

The Three M's are the foundation you build your tax business on. They are the three-legged marketing stool from which your core tax business promotions come. If one of the Three M's doesn't measure up, the stool falls over and your campaign is toast.

Market ... Message ... Media

Let's start with MARKET. Now everybody's heard the term "target market." The problem is very few tax pros can describe in detail "who" their target market is. And if a tax business owner CAN describe their target market to me, there's usually no intentional and purposeful marketing plan currently being used to TARGET this group.

So before you decide on a particular strategy for marketing your tax business, the first, most important question you must answer is, WHO?

Who is most likely to want to do business with your tax practice based on all the other tax-related service options out there?

There are so many people in your market area that need help filing their taxes. And we both know you can do any and all of those tax returns. But just because you can, doesn't mean you should. When you put yourself out there as being everything to everybody, you'll actually reduce your response rates.

Your tax business marketing has to zero in like a laser and target one, two, three or a small handful of specific markets who, when coming across your ad, will say, "Hey, that's for me. I'm calling them right now."

BLOCKBUSTER
How To Build A Million Dollar Tax Business

The second M is MESSAGE. It answers the question, WHY? **Why in the world should somebody in your market area (or online) choose you?** (Having the same answer as your competition is NOT going to cut it.) Have you given them a reason?

Here's what happens. Most people who get into the tax business just hang out a shingle saying, "I do tax returns" and hope for the best. Maybe they think, "I'm going to be over on this side of town because there are no tax businesses over here. I'll just open up shop and see how it goes." Or another tax pro will take the opposite approach and say, "Oh, well, the brand name competition is there, so I'm going to go open an office right next to them because that's where the people who pay for tax preparation services are going."

I understand both of these strategies, but that's still not answering the very important question of message. You MUST be able to articulate to your target market why they should choose you compared to the CPA across the street, or the National Tax Franchise downtown, or even that independent tax firm who's been in business for decades right down the road.

Note: Don't forget you need to answer the question, "Why should your target market choose you versus filing their taxes online themselves?" Taxpayers think they can do a good job, but you and I both know they're nuts to try and go it alone with Uncle Sam these days. They're way better off calling you, but you haven't given them any GREAT reasons to do so in your marketing.

Actually, <u>you'll want to give multiple reasons for your target market to choose you over all the other options available to them. These reasons are called your Unique Selling Propositions (or USP's).</u> **You stack these USP's up in your promotional campaign and make an irresistible offer your target market can't refuse!**

Properly crafted, your tax business's USP's ANSWER the "why" question.

The third M (or leg) of this three-legged marketing stool is MEDIA. It answers the question HOW. How are you going to deliver your promotion to a specific group of taxpayers? (Your target market – The Who.)

Now MEDIA can take many forms of advertising vehicles. Media can be standing up and speaking at an event or even a luncheon. Media can be putting an ad in a local newspaper. It can be TV, radio -- all forms of mass broadcasts. Obviously, direct mail, email, websites are media. Banners, billboards, signs, flyers, social media and online videos are all forms of media. The point is there are MANY different ways to deliver your marketing message and there are pros and cons to all of them.

Since I'm a direct response marketing consultant, I want to measure and track what kinds of adverting work and don't work. I always want to hold my marketing accountable. Direct response media has to be able to deliver the message to (reach) a particular target group effectively and affordably.

I want to know my Return On Investment (ROI) with every media I use so I can decide whether it's wise for me to re-do the marketing campaign or not. The trick is to find multiple different media sources that all yield an acceptable range of ROI so you can out-spend your competition. If you can afford to invest more in your tax business's marketing campaigns than your competitors, you will "steal" more than your fair share of new tax clients in your area.

Do You Advertise Your Tax Business Like This?

This is what normally happens when a tax business owner decides to advertise. Before many tax pros run an ad, they will sit down in front of their computer. First thing they type in is their name or the name of their business – right at the top. Next they probably put something like "Taxes" or "Need Tax Help?" After that, they'll add, "I've been in the business 20 years and here's my contact information. I'm located over here. Here's my website." Basically, the ad looks like a business card. What's sad is the fact that almost every tax firm in town has a similar ad.

What I'm trying to get across to you is profoundly simple. **You must differentiate your tax business.** (So FEW tax pros do this well.) You have got to set yourself apart. You must have a reason that makes your tax practice different in a compelling way.

Remember, you're looking to set yourself apart for your target market (not every Tom, Dick, and Harry trying to file their taxes). You want to clearly differentiate yourself to the people that are most likely to want to do business with you. That means some of your ads will turn folks off, but at the same time, attract the taxpayers you want to do business with the most.

That's what really good marketing does. Repel people that are not a good match for your business and attract the ones who are.

Systems

Let's talk about the INSIDE of your tax office. What's your strategy for office flow?

The best way to efficiently and effectively take care of your clients inside your tax office is to focus on two areas: *Your People and Your Processes.* Recruiting and hiring good people can make a lot of wrong things right in your office. But I'm only going to cover PROCESS right now. (I'll talk about PEOPLE later in this book.)

Your Process consists of a series of Systems. A System is nothing more than a checklist. A checklist gives specific steps (Step 1, Step 2, Step 3, Step 4, Step 5, etc.) in a correct order. Your goal is to ensure your office procedures are followed the same way over and over again. This greatly improves operations inside your office and causes things to flow the way you (the owner) want them to flow.

When I do in-office operational consultations for tax businesses, for simplicity's sake, I like to break down each tax office into a Front, Middle and Back.

What most tax pros do is look at other tax businesses' layout, and model their office accordingly. You know, a table here, a reception area there; then add a couple of chairs and desks; include a partition here, a little plant there, a couple of computers in the middle towards the back – and don't forget the conference table in the meeting room. Most tax offices look the same. That's fine, IF **you have an operations plan and purpose to maximize profits and give your clients a "talk-about-you-to-their-friends" experience.** Most tax business owners have no plan and no profit strategy for the internal side of their practice.

So what do you do? How does a tax business owner get an Operations Plan for their tax office? Ask and then answer this simple question, **"What does success look like inside my tax office?"** I'm talking about operational success. What's the flow? What's supposed to happen when the client walks in the door? In a best-case scenario, what's going to happen from start to finish with each client?

YOU KNOW THE ANSWER TO THIS QUESTION. (Plus, this book will give you dozens of additional ideas to help you improve your answers even more.)

For now, start with what you know. Take out your smart phone and go stand outside your office. Push record and start talking. Describe in a best-case scenario what you'd like to see happen EVERY time a client walks into your tax office.

This will be the genesis of articulating what success looks like to any old or new employee working for you fulltime, part-time or just seasonally.

I recommend you record your thoughts (audio) with visual clarity (video) in two or three minute segments. Get as specific as you can. Your words will be transcribed and formed into a series of steps. These steps will make up the Systems. And the Systems will link together for a successful process that guarantees you MUCH IMPROVEMENT in whatever you're doing now in your office operationally.

So if we're talking about the FRONT of the office, what should your lobby look like in the best-case scenario? What should happen when the client comes in and is greeted? What if they are a walk-in, someone with an appointment or even a drop off?

You should systematically go through *every inch* of your tax office and get something recorded and then documented. It's not that hard to describe all the different things you want to see happen in YOUR office. After you've transcribed the audio and let your staff watch the video, GET THEM TO FILL IN THE BLANKS ON ANYTHING YOU MISSED. It helps them buy in to this process of improving the overall operational flow of the office.

In your tax office, what should you do with the MIDDLE of your office? Is that where the tax preparation desks should be? What about the BACK of your tax business? Should you have staff reviewing tax returns, fixing errors or even processing paperwork?

The truth is, it's up to you to decide what you want to do where. The only criteria are: *"Will this make us more efficient? Will we take care of clients better? Will this office set-up maximize our profits?"*

What I just described to you is a real-world solution to improving your tax office operations. You will continuously focus on improvement, always looking to reduce stress, headaches and office flow problems.

80/20 Rule Strategies

Tax business owners have a tendency to treat all of their clients the same way. This would be a mistake because not all clients are "equal" when it comes to running a successful tax practice. A long-time, high-paying client should receive more time and attention from you versus a brand new person walking into your office seeking help with a basic 1040.

A more common scenario I see played out is a tax pro spending the same amount of money on outbound communications with Client X (first time client who filed a $200 tax return a couple of months ago) and Client Y (a client who has entrusted you with their growing business for five years and pays you $2,000 annually.) Now, I'm NOT talking about treating Client X and

BLOCKBUSTER
How To Build A Million Dollar Tax Business

Client Y differently in regards to respect and courtesy. Of course you will honor ALL of the people who come to you for tax help no matter how much money they pay you for their services.

But you are only one person. And whoever you have working for you can only do so much for your clients, too. There are limitations we all have to deal with. So in order to properly provide a higher level of service to your high-value clients (monetarily) you must go through a process of prioritizing your client list.

Set up the criteria however you want. Dollar per return, highest margins per service, longevity per year, ease of doing business, etc. Now you'll be able to divide your clients into an A List, B List, C List and finally a D List.

The A List has your BEST clients. And the D List represents the five to ten percent of your clients who cause most of your problems, giving you the most stress and worse, bringing you little-to-no profit.

[Hint: Your D List needs to be dumped.]

Give them to your competition (seriously), or sell them. A third option is increasing your fees by 300 percent for your D List and let them go or stay. If they stay, they will be better behaved clients and you'll obviously make more money.

So why go to all the trouble to separate out your client list? The short answer is the universal law we've all heard of: The 80/20 Rule.

The bad part is, every tax pro on the planet has heard of 80/20 for business. But VERY few tax business owners actually run their operations based on the 80/20 Rule.

BLOCKBUSTER
How To Build A Million Dollar Tax Business

To be strategic with the 80/20 Rule, you must spend your time and money differently. If you are serious about massive tax business growth, chances are good that 80 percent of how you spend your time in your business right now needs to be changed. Since you are the owner, you should be focused (mostly) on highly-leveraged opportunities which will likely bring many more new clients and high-margin revenue to your business. Usually, the tax business owner does the opposite and only 20 percent of your time is spent on activities that are most likely to grow your business and make you more successful.

We've already talked about your client list and how to structure the list to increase your profits and reduce your stress and headaches. This IS a Basic 80/20 Rule Strategy, and if properly executed, you can DOUBLE your profits in one tax season.

How? Because if you actually invest more time and money into your best clients, you WILL make more money.

If you dramatically reduce or eliminate your worst clients who suck 80 percent of your time and energy, a space vacuum will occur. Once opened, the natural word of mouth trend from your client list will draw more well-matched taxpayers to you from your A and B Lists because more of your focus and attention were placed there. (It's amazing how word of mouth spreads and GOOD clients fill in the space vacuum once held by BAD clients who are now gone.)

So what are the highest payoff priorities in your office? **If you could only focus your attention on 20 percent of the activities which brought in 80 percent of your net profit, wouldn't that be easier and a more effective way to make more money?**

What if we just focused on the top ten areas inside your tax office you feel need the most improvement and would best contribute to your tax business's bottom line. Now, let's stick with our 80/20 Rule theme. Narrow your focus to ONLY your top two or three, which is about twenty percent.

(Note: You probably are overwhelmed with the idea of "changing" everything in your tax office to become more successful. Good news: If you update and dramatically improve your top two or three, you could see an eighty percent improvement on what's most important to you in your business.)

If I'm in your shoes, these would be my top three priorities:

- Develop Irresistible Offer Inside A Compelling Ad Promoting Your Tax Biz

- Steward Inbound Phone Calls (turn taxpayer inquiries into office appointments)

- Assume The Sale of Additional Services (extra profit on top of tax prep services)

We will cover these three areas in detail later in this book.

Break Through Your Ceiling

Every tax business hits a ceiling. The question is, **what are you going to do to break through YOUR ceiling?**

Usually bottlenecks inside your business are the culprit. For some reason, marketing and advertising stops. Quality employees don't get recruited or hired. Work flow sits in piles, waiting for completion. The new ideas or suggestions from the staff rarely get implemented.

What's causing these bottlenecks?

Let's be honest. Every tax business owner must look in the mirror. Acknowledging the truth about their role in the business and the lack of success and/or unfulfilled dreams is the first step towards freedom ... and breaking through that unwanted ceiling hanging over the tax business.

Let's say you're doing $250,000 in gross sales and you'd really like to get to that $500,000 mark. Well, chances are, if you're going to double your business like that, you're going to have to *STOP doing* some things and *START doing* others.

It's realistic that you'll probably need to hire another person to come in and do some of the tasks in your business you might not like to do or be good at. I'm not good at plenty of things, and I hire people all the time to help me because I know my strengths and I hire out the rest.

Tax business owners have a tendency to use the "I can't find a quality person" excuse. But the truth is: good people are easy to find! They're all over the place. Just run compelling recruiting ads (Hint: don't make them look like everyone else's "help wanted" ads), and allow the candidates to show you their quality by asking them to perform several specific action steps in your ad. The ones who "jump through these hoops" are perfect prospects for you to speak with and eventually hire.

Now, if you are going to double your revenue, I believe it's a safe bet to say you'll need to delegate more. If you've had bad experiences delegating in the past and you're not willing to do it anymore (this is a CEILING holding you back all by itself), then you probably were dumping projects on your employees and not using proper delegating techniques. This is easy to fix. (Keep reading ... I'll cover this topic soon.)

BLOCKBUSTER
How To Build A Million Dollar Tax Business

Making Good Ads Work Better

What most tax business owners do when it comes to marketing their practice is promote their tax services using what I call "the business card look" ad. In 99 percent of the cases, the ad doesn't work. And since most tax pros treat marketing as an expense, what's the first thing that gets cut when an accountant tries to save money? Right – marketing!

Later, when someone asks them how they promote their practice, the answer is usually, "We do word-of-mouth marketing." (Translation: I can't figure out how to turn a profit when I spend money on advertising our tax business, so I'm just going to ask my clients to tell their friends about us and hope for the best.)

But what if you DO have an ad that works for your tax business? And you do your best to track the results and you feel very comfortable spending more money on that same ad over and over again? Think – how do you make more money with this promotion?

Well, one of my best tricks is to focus on the two most important pieces of the ad: The *Headline* and the *Offer*. When I provide ad critiques for my Real Tax Business Success Members, I write a more powerful, attention grabbing headline that will get more eyeballs to read the ad. If the ad works, it will work even better now. Then, because most tax business ads are timid when it comes asking for response to the promotion, I usually beef up the "call to action" (another way to say *Offer*) and get those who were on the fence to call or go to the tax business' website.

<u>The other way to boost profits from an Ad that's working is to FIND ANOTHER POND TO GO FISHING IN. That means if your ad worked for one target group, then in all likelihood, you</u>

can tweak the ad and run the promo for another target group. (ie. Fish in a different pond.)

I do this ALL the time. And I believe more tax business owners should follow this simple strategy and leverage what they already have working and find another media and/or target list to run their marketing campaign over and over again.

Plus, a secret most tax business owners miss is strategically connecting the regular marketing promotions for their tax office (offline) with an effective ONLINE tax business marketing campaign. This includes a direct response website, a relationship-building email funnel, and a social media platform to spread word-of-mouth.

If interested in more Internet Marketing Best Practices for Tax Firms, go here:

www.MillionDollarTaxBiz.com/OnlineMarketing

More Referrals

Every tax business owner gets referrals. You are in a service business. You BETTER be getting people to refer you!

But here's how you can grow the number of referrals you are getting now.

Build a *Culture of Referrals*. Make it clear to everyone walking into your tax office: referring your friends, neighbors and co-workers is what we do here.

Once your 'culture' has been established, at the same time you must also formulize a *Referral System*. Don't just say, "Hey, please tell your friends about us."

Instead, strategically document and systemize your whole referral program and your referral results will skyrocket!

Make it magnetic: add colored fliers, record videos of your best clients talking about how great it is to refer, feature those families who refer your tax business the most on your Facebook page and even in your monthly newsletter. Have some fun with it!

But most of all, SCHEDULE your Refer-A-Friend campaign BEFORE, DURING and AFTER your clients come into your office for tax season. By pre-choosing actual dates in the calendar and promoting your incentives, contests and whatever else you want to do, this extra communication will win over your clients, causing a bushfire of referral activity.

WHEN YOU SYSTEMIZE YOUR REFERRAL PROCESS (BEFORE, DURING AND AFTER A CLIENT LEAVES YOUR OFFICE) IT WILL BOOST YOUR OVERALL WORD-OF-MOUTH AWARENESS TO THE PEOPLE MOST LIKELY TO TELL OTHERS ABOUT YOUR TAX BUSINESS.

I know it's a lot of extra work, but it's worth it. I promise!

The Economics of Your Tax Business

Everybody's heard – Cash is King. Well, to get to the cash, you gotta do THE MATH!

In Tax Business Success Economics, if you don't get the numbers right, much of what you move forward with is doomed to fail. You see, I've watched many well-intentioned tax pros try to grow their business to the next level, but they ended up getting stuck and losing money. They never figured out where to start, what numbers to crunch, what dollar percentages they needed to pay attention to or even basic management formulas to follow.

Most tax business owners think they know their numbers off the top of their head. But the truth is you must measure and track your numbers more closely and consistently if you want to be successful.

Start by compiling a baseline figure of whatever areas of your tax business you see as most important for reaching your goals. A basic strategic plan will have goals attached to it. And the glue that keeps you on track to achieving your goals and completing a successful strategic plan is IMPLEMENTATION. (This word is tied to your success more than any other word.) And the only way to truly implement your tax business success plan is to track and measure THE NUMBERS so you know where you stand each day, week or month.

Now Strategy IS important, too! There are many ways to reach a particular goal for your tax business. But your goals must be clear and feasible to achieve. If you can work backwards on THE MATH, and notice pathways to reach your goals, you'll be well on your way. Also, the daily and weekly discipline of tracking your results helps focus your efforts and direct your path if you get off course.

The Bottom Line:
Do you care HOW you reach your income goals?

One of the fastest, simplest ways your tax business can improve on the economic front is in your price list. Eighty percent of the tax industry (nationwide) is UNDER-priced. Just ask the national tax firms what they do when they buy an independent tax firm. They immediately double the fees. And even if half of these clients don't return, the new tax firm still makes more net profit. Do the math.

So eight of ten tax firms in your city are leaving money on the table. Are you one of them?

No matter where you think you are on price (high, low or just right), I recommend you take a look at INCREASING your fees. Evaluate different forms and review what you charge. Which forms do you think need adjusting? Fix those now. In most cases, you're too low on 80 percent of your forms. If I were you, I'd double my prices. Seriously.

<u>Years ago I got so fed up with the stress and hassles of tax season, and I said to my dad, "If we're gonna go through all of these headaches during tax season, we need a lot more money in our bank account on April 16 ... I suggest we double our prices next year."</u>

The cool part of the story was we DID increase our prices by 100 percent and prepared/filed taxes for the same number of clients as the previous year (actually a little more). But the massive increase in NET PROFIT was a wake-up call to me. We increased our fees each year for five more years until we hit the double mark again! (By the way, during these years, the volume of clients we serviced increased 10-to-30 percent EACH YEAR depending on the year.)

TAKE A SERIOUS LOOK AT THE SERVICES YOU OFFER

The last issue I want to address here is "finding your dogs." Just analyze your numbers and see which of your services are underperforming. Every tax firm in America has stuff they do that's not good for the business's bottom line. These services need to STOP. You do them out of habit or whatever. But at the end of the day, these services are COSTING YOU time and money because they take away from the more profitable, higher margin services you know you'd like to do more of.

By the same token, you've got to add some new services, too. If you're just in the tax preparation business, that's not good. Most tax firms have additional services they provide because there's a lot more money to be made in the tax business besides preparation. You know this, but maybe you got lazy and didn't pursue other financial options to offer your clients. JUST LOOK AT YOUR CLIENTS' NUMBERS. Many times their tax returns will point you to exactly what you need to begin offering.

Somebody's going to sell your clients additional financial related services. It might as well be you. You have the relationship with them. You've built the trust factor. Now pay attention to the economic opportunities right under your nose!

If you follow these simple but powerful secrets – you WILL dramatically help your tax business get to the next level. They are simple. This is NOT rocket science. The key is execution of these strategies.

In other words ... JUST DO THEM!

Chapter 4

Top 10 Best Questions To Ask ... (Then Answer) For Your Tax Biz

Over the last couple of decades, I've done a lot of speaking. Whether it's a presentation at one of my events, another tax industry seminar, or an IRS Forum, I get asked a ton of questions by tax business owners as soon as I walk off the stage. Some are good questions. Others not so much. So I decided to give you the top questions I'd ask if I were in your shoes today, plus the answers to better help your tax practice.

Question #1

How should I differentiate my tax business from all other competitors so that I'm positioned as the best option when choosing a tax professional?

You MUST have a reason why taxpayers are going to choose you over many other tax filing options available to them. To do this, you develop a Unique Selling Proposition. I call it a USP for short.

You might have one, two, three or more USP's. They are all differentiators which set you apart so you don't look like a commodity. At the very least, your tax business has to have one reason why a prospect that is well-matched to benefit from the services your tax practice offers will choose you over your competition. Once you answer this question (well), you are now in the driver's seat to begin promoting your tax business.

A quality Unique Selling Proposition is a springboard to many other marketing messages, advertising hooks or ways to grab the attention of your target market. This is foundational.

By the way, **I don't recommend that you try to be all things to all people.**

Of course you can prepare everybody's tax return, but that's not the point. When you advertise yourself, you want a certain segment of the population in your area to say, "Hey, that's for me." When they come across your attention-getting headline, read your ad, listen to you on the radio, see your TV spot, or go online and click on your website, no matter what, it's very important for the target person you want as a client to feel like you are in the tax business for them.

How do you do that?

One way is to target a niche market. A niche could be an occupation. A niche could be a geographic area.

A niche could be a certain profile of income, married with multiple kids. There's a lot of different ways to slice and dice it. And usually, you're going to have more than one niche.

If you're not sure about WHO you should target, just look at your existing client base. See who's already doing business with you. You've probably been advertising like a generalist anyway. (ninety-nine percent of tax pros do this.) Over the years, through word-of-mouth and referrals, people have come to you for tax help and now you've got a client list.

But in EVERY list, there are commonalities. So by accident you will have small groups of like-minded people (niches) who are already happy and excited to have you as their tax preparer or accountant. They like each other, they talk to one another, and better yet, they refer each other to your tax business. That's a great sign.

Maybe you have a bunch of nurses or teachers or dog lovers or golfers or whoever. Could these be possible hungry markets in your area? Be proactive towards these particular niches and get testimonials from your existing clients to help you testify about how great your tax services are.

Using the dog-lover niche example:

Include a picture of the dog and write copy about how your tax office is dog-friendly and how the tax pro financially supports dog related causes in the local area. Can you see how your tax business would set itself apart from other tax pros in the area (in a good way) if your ads were targeted to dog lovers? This type of a strategy would be one of your Unique Selling Propositions.

Another differentiator that sets you apart from your competition is YOUR story. You have a unique story. Your background and 'what makes you tick' truly helps your Unique Selling Proposition. Most tax pros tell me they don't have an "exciting" story. This is baloney. As soon as I start asking them questions about their life, what they are interested in, what they like to do for fun, all kinds of STORYLINES come to the surface.

Truth be told, if you shared your hobbies, family activities and trips you take with friends or relatives, you'd be shocked how much you have in common with many of your clients. And the cool part is that most taxpayers searching for help with filing their taxes are ATTRACTED to parts of your story, much more so than the letters behind your name or your years of experience in the tax industry.

(I can't tell you how many tax pros just don't get what I just said.)

STORY MATTERS!

Telling parts of your story in various marketing campaigns sets you apart from the other BORING tax business ads which are circulated during tax season, and all look the same. You do NOT want to get lumped into the "boring group" when spending your promotional dollars growing your tax business.

Question #2
How do you make more profit per tax client?

This is a great question because a lot of tax pros don't ask this question early on in the life of their business. Most tax business owners are way too low when it comes to pricing the services they provide. The reason the majority of the tax professionals in the United States aren't making the money they hope for comes down to this issue: *Profit Margins.* The fees tax pros charge are just too low. It's that simple.

The first (quick) answer to this problem is raising your prices. I'm serious. This is the most obvious way to add significant profit to your bottom line. But the first (and worst) push back will come from the thoughts that happen right between your ears.

Yes, increase your fees. Don't make any excuses. No apologies needed. Of course you'll catch a little heat from a handful of your clients. Oh, well – they probably needed to find a new tax pro anyway, right? Truth is, your tax business will NET a lot more money once the whiners, complainers and cheapskates get out of your business anyway. Just do the math. You'll make more money and you'll enjoy tax season much more after the "bad apples" are out.

The second strategy for making more profit per client is bundling some of your services together.

I like recommending year-round memberships. You can include tax preparation and other financial related services throughout the off season. Most of these services you might not charge for, but you should. But by bundling them in with your core services, you add tremendous value for your client; they become a better client and you get paid HIGHER fees. In addition, most of these extra services will NOT be used by the client each year. And since you didn't have to invest your time in providing these services, you will enjoy HIGHER margins as well.

The last (but not least) strategy for increasing your profit is offering some kind of audit insurance. I wouldn't even up-sell it. I would ASSUME THE SALE and add it to your fees as part of your services – that means EVERYONE who files a tax return with you.

I have tax business owners in my Real Tax Business Success Membership Group who've used this strategy by charging as little as an extra $39 per tax return. I have other tax pro clients charging $69, $99 and even hundreds of dollars depending on the type of tax return they are preparing. You definitely want to add this kind of service to your tax preparation to protect YOU and YOUR CLIENT.

BLOCKBUSTER
How To Build A Million Dollar Tax Business

IRS letters are on the rise and will continue to hassle taxpayers for many years to come. Historically speaking, most tax business owners do NOT charge their client for answering a question or providing more info for Uncle Sam when an IRS letter is brought to their attention in the off season. Now you'll get paid whether Uncle Sam mails your client a letter or not.

Don't keep saying, "Well, making a few phone calls to the IRS in the summer for my client is part of my service for filing the taxes." This may be true, but the practice is killing your margins during a twelve month sales cycle.

Adding a self-insured audit protection plan to EVERY tax client in your tax business allows you to decide what forms you will (AND WILL NOT) include in this service. (Don't go through some third party!) You charge what you want, provide whatever level of protection you want and enjoy significant NET increase to your bottom line each year!

Question #3
How do I attract quality new clients best matched for my tax business target market?

This is marketing 101. Do you have a target market? Are you intentional about seeking out a particular type of taxpayer(s) for your tax practice? How do you attract quality new clients that are best matched for your tax business? Well, you have to start with a profile: Who these people are, and even more importantly, WHO THEY ARE NOT!

If you're not sure how best to describe the best target client for your tax business, try this. Think about your top ten favorite clients.

BLOCKBUSTER
How To Build A Million Dollar Tax Business

They give you whatever you need to provide your services in a timely manner. They are easy to work with. They never give you any trouble. Their tax returns are very high profit with very nice margins on additional services. They pay you fast. They're thrilled with your service. They think you can "walk on water."

Every tax business owner can point to some folks in their list like this. Write their names down. Pull out a sheet of paper (for each of these ten clients) and describe what you know about all of them in as much detail as you can.

At some point, you'll find crossover characteristics. There will be a few interesting commonalities. You'll see matching pieces of a puzzle pop off the page at you. THESE WILL BE THE FOUNDATIONS OF A PROFILE FOR YOUR PERFECT CLIENT. From this information, you will now be able to define the best target market(s) for your tax business.

Next, I'd recommend you go find other businesses or organizations with the same target clientele. They may be high income or low income, adventurous outdoors types or inside computer gamers, single moms with kids or retired couples with no one else at home.

My point is, birds of a feather flock together, so look around where YOUR target market lives, works or participates in weekly/monthly activities. And if you don't know, ASK THEM. (Simple but effective surveys are easy to send out by email.)

At the end of the day, you'll KNOW what these people WANT.

<u>So as part of your marketing MESSAGE, you will craft their "wants" into your Unique Selling Proposition. That will make your USP act like a magnet, attracting the exact type of clients best suited for your tax business.</u>

Question #4

How do I systemize my tax office's workflow without the majority of our tax services running through me?

Does your tax office run this way? I see this problem all the time. In a typical tax practice, way too much of the workload goes through the owner. And guess what? It's the owner's fault!

The tax business owner feels like they must have their fingers in everything. Got to "look" at everything and make sure everything is "right" WAY too much of the time. (It's called control. Sometimes masked as perfectionism.) If you're this behavioral style, that's ok. There are plenty of things you can do to take a healthier approach. But you must be willing to take a SERIOUS look at making some changes.

Note: It's for your own good. If you continue down this road of needing to control everything, you'll never be able to break through the revenue cap sealed over your business. YOU are the person stopping your business from growing and making money.

The obvious way to begin fixing this issue is to hire a few good employees. And by the way, people make mistakes just like you, so it's not like we're out trying to hire perfection. There are PLENTY of quality individuals with excellent experience waiting for you to interview them.

You hire one or two, train them on a few specific projects and then follow up at the agreed upon time to review their work. You'll build trust with them in a matter of weeks or months so they'll be able to do higher level projects for you. You are not going to just dump work on an individual and hope they do it "like you want." You'll lead your tax business by example, showing real delegation where there's a real follow-up effective process.

BLOCKBUSTER
How To Build A Million Dollar Tax Business

Let's say preparing tax returns is the core project. Remember The 80/20 Rule? An example of 80/20 would be 80 percent of your tax returns really can be reviewed by a less experienced employee who knows how to do tax returns, and checks for common errors. They know enough to know when a return is right and when there is a chance of an error because the return is above their experience level. Those returns (about 20 percent) go into a pile for a more experienced preparer to review.

The point is THE OWNER shouldn't have to touch 80 percent of these returns in the review process. Now, the other 20 percent ... sure, let the owner's eyeballs hit those if you don't already have a super experienced person helping with this task. The reason I share this type of example is to underscore how eliminating this kind of bottleneck is NOT difficult. The same is true with many other bottlenecks in your tax office.

If I could ask employees of many tax firms scattered across the country to answer freely (without fear of the owner finding out) what is the main operational problem in the business, the answer 80 percent of the time would be the owner.

Look, a true SYSTEM inside your office is a clear process, from beginning to end which (from my view point) does NOT involve the owner. As the leader of my tax practice, my job is to make sure "all systems are go" and each department of my office runs smoothly. If I'm IN the process, I can't see or lead everything else.

Of course, there are plenty of exceptions when you are a small operation and the owner has to do more of the heavy lifting. But that doesn't mean you have to stay that way!

Finally, success in this area becomes a reality when the owner WINS mentally. A mental shift must take place for most owners to move forward. If everything continues to go through you, how much can you really grow? Seriously.

The owner (unknowingly) acts like an iron-clad lock on his or her bank account, keeping it shut from growing and expanding. You cannot grow your tax practice to the next level if you are not dealing with this issue in a real way. You must let go of (at least) SOME of the daily, weekly tasks and let other people do some work for you. If not, you can't do what's necessary to let the business grow to a new level.

Question #5
How do I hire employees with salesmanship gifts and then train them in tax knowledge, which is a skill needed for their position?

Now, some people don't even agree with the premise of this question. But it's true. Most tax businesses lack basic salesmanship skills. It's much easier to hire a sales person and teach them about taxes than it is to hire an experienced tax preparer and make them a sales person.

Since we are in a SERVICE business, building rapport with clients and expressing empathy for their tax situation is much more valuable than tax pros realize. Obviously it's important to file a correct tax return (don't get me wrong -- tax prep is a core service.) But your growth will continue at a snail's pace if you don't add a little gas to your tax business' engine.

The owner needs to 'buy into' a salesmanship philosophy inside his or her own tax office. If your tax business is in growth mode, I recommend hiring retail type employees that you train on basic tax prep in early tax season. These folks like to sell, they like to talk to people and they have friendly, bubbly personalities.

The timing is perfect because they want to continue working. They probably just finished the Christmas season and now want a different kind of experience. Many times they are great with helping fill-in-the-gaps where they are most needed in your office. Most will find other jobs in the spring season. You might also give a raise to the best seasonal employee you hired and keep them on year-round for more training and growth within your company.

Question #6

What is the best advertising and marketing media I can invest in for growing my tax business?

That's a loaded question; there's really no good answer. The real answer is you've got to test each ad and every marketing campaign. Of course, everyone wants a magic bullet. They'll say, "Hey, give me one ad," and they'll run it all over the place and all these new clients will come in and the office will be overwhelmed with business. That's not reality.

The truth is, you're going to need to run multiple different types of ads, work through multiple kinds of media and strategically connect several messages (depending on the timing of tax season) and at the same time TRACK the results so you know where to leverage your marketing dollars and where to pull the plug. Contrary to popular belief, not all of your ads will work.

Also, you do NOT want to participate in brand advertising or brand building. That's ridiculous. You don't have the money or the time for that. For regular small-to mid-sized businesses, direct-response marketing is THE way to go. All of your ads and marketing campaigns become measurable and trackable, which means your marketing dollars are held accountable.

Question #7
What are my core competencies I enjoy and want to continue doing in my tax business and what business responsibilities do I delegate?

You need to do what you like to do in your business. The problem is, if your competency is preparing tax returns, and that's all you do, you'll never grow to a million-dollar tax business. You will have to limit the number of tax returns you do. You'll need to cherry pick the ones you like, and delegate the rest because, truth be told, you ARE the owner. And if the majority of your day is providing "basic service" work (IN your business, not ON your business) then you're not going to grow to the level you desire.

As the owner, you are the rainmaker. You're responsible for bringing in business. If on a typical day you are participating in "production work" in the context of your office flow – then this is a problem because ultimately, you are losing money overall.

Delegation should be your middle name. It's okay to do something once or twice. But the employees working for you should know enough about your business matrix to realize that you (the owner) should NOT be on the "front line" of your tax practice. You can't have your eyes lowered on the daily workload in the forest, when your head must stay above the tree line, able to steer your business to better opportunities.

Quick Tip:
Since you're The Boss, on many occasions your tax business problems tend to float back up river and fall into your lap. Here's how to cut back on this hassle and time sucking occurrence.

Hire what I call Shield Staff.

This person (or it can be multiple employees who take turns) is someone that everybody comes to with the problems of the office. They used to come to the owner, but now we have a "Shield Staff" Member who drops whatever they are doing and fixes whatever the problem is. Properly trained, in most cases this person will handle eight out of ten questions or issues that arise. That's great, because now you're only dealing with 20 percent of the stress and headaches that you dealt with before. And let me tell you this: once you get used to having a BUFFER to protect you from the normal day-to-day problems, you will never go back to this kind of frontline stress – especially during tax season.

Question #8
What business organizations with similar clients can you leverage for an ongoing win-win Joint Venture?

Many tax pros don't even know what a Joint Venture is, so let me just explain this term first. Joint Venture is nothing more than making a win-win situation with another business owner or organization.

You want to jointly work with each other so both of your companies benefit. If you're looking to get more new clients and they want to leverage their customer list, then you have an excellent way to work on a promotional campaign together to accomplish each other's goals.

An excellent place to look for Joint Venture (JV) opportunities is within your own client base. Why? Because it's best to enter into a JV with businesses or organizations who service similar clients or customers as your tax practice. Just ask your clients where they shop, where they go for recreation or even to list their favorite hobbies.

It's not a whole lot of effort, but most tax pros miss this base because they don't take the time to go across the street to a similar business, or talk to other owners with the same kind of clientele. Most other business owners are very open to listening to an idea that would get them more clients or more money, especially if you're doing the majority of the work for them.

What many tax pros don't understand is the new clients they get from the other business participating in the JV are their BEST customers! How do I know? Well, they responded to your offer based off the endorsement of the other business owner. These new clients don't know you from Adam's house cat. They are BUYERS. That means once you do a great job helping them with filing their taxes, they are much more likely to buy additional services you offer them in the future.

Question #9
How can I build my relationships with my clients on an ongoing basis so they'll never leave and they'll refer new clients to my tax business like crazy?

This one is easy. You tell your story and have some fun. Just don't be boring.

Don't be boring, boring, boring like every other tax professional in your area.

Smile. A lot.

Be purposeful about taking care of your clients. Communicate on a regular basis with your clients. Use different themes currently in the news. Issues you like to talk about. Stuff you're interested in.

Then continue to build this persona of you being a regular person (just be yourself) and, oh by the way, you happen to be an expert at taxes.

Question #10

How can I increase my personal wealth by offering some additional products and services to my clients?

There is truly a lot you can do in this area.

But here's the main thing you want to keep in mind. On a regular basis, ask your clients what YOU can DO to make their life easier, better or happier. Actively reaching out to your clients on a year-round basis will continually build trust in your relationship. Most tax pros just prepare the tax return, catch up for a few minutes and then see them the following tax season.

When you stay connected, you learn much more about what your clients actually want – especially your best clients. Based on their feedback, you'll find products and services with low and medium and high price points to offer them on a monthly or quarterly basis. Since you are a tax professional, you can tell the story of why these various services and products should be purchased from you as their tax advisor.

I would highly recommend you customize some of these offers to specific niches you specialize in. You can put together trips or vacations and facilitate clients meeting and even do business together. There are plenty of out-of-the-box ideas you can implement, which sets you apart as a tax professional that'll never be considered boring. You'll be positioned as a cutting-edge financial professional helping other people grow to the next level of their life -- leaving your competition in the dirt.

BLOCKBUSTER
How To Build A Million Dollar Tax Business

How do I take my tax business to a higher level of success?

Well, success is relative. So decide what success looks like for you. If success is adding an extra hundred tax returns this year, great. Let's figure out the math and the strategy on how to do that. If success is adding $500,000 in revenue to your multi-location tax firm, no problem. We can do that, too.

I had a coaching client years ago. His definition of success for the upcoming tax season was, "I want to be home eating dinner with my family by seven o'clock every night this tax season." That was his definition of success. It didn't have anything to do with money. His business was fine. He just was driving himself bonkers by working way too many hours during tax season and getting home at midnight too many weeks (which turned into months) and this schedule just wore him out. He knew life was too short to continue at this pace.

So whether it's just the amount of work that you do, or it's the amount of money you make, define what success looks like for you. Find an expert with specialized knowledge on showing you exactly what to do.

I help tax pros define what success looks like on a regular basis. They enroll in one of my coaching programs and I help them move from "stuck" to thriving. Way too many tax business owners STAY stuck year after year, not seeing the progress in their business they know should be there.

Success is not rocket science.

Get the right person to walk alongside your business and give you the short-cuts to help get you over the hump.

If you don't stop, you win.

Chapter 5

Advanced Tax Biz Marketing Reinvent What You Do

I don't know of any tax business that wouldn't like a shot-in-the-arm jolt of new energy and excitement, generating additional revenue streams for their business.

For something like this to happen (in a big way), you must seriously consider revamping everything you do. When it comes to promoting, marketing and advertising your tax business, there are many connecting points inside and outside of your business.

Adding new processes and adjusting others (whether you realize they're happening in your business or not) is mandatory for these new marketing campaigns and advertising funnels to work.

Change is good.

Most people don't like change, but change really is a good thing. Some tax pros are forced into change and they don't like it. But once they get to the other side of this unsettling season, they're able to look back and say, "Wow! That was good. It was kind of a pain at the time ... and I didn't like it when I was going through it, but we are a better business because we transitioned through that change."

So, instead of being forced into it, which is how many tax pros deal with the changes in their business, what if you were proactive? Getting ahead of the curve and beating your competition to the place both of you WILL be going in the near future is better for you and your business, I promise!

Okay, now let me start off by giving you my SIMPLE definition of marketing.

Marketing is getting a particular type of person who is most likely to want to do business with you to raise their hand and say, "I'm interested."

Some business "experts" say brand building is very important to marketing. I don't agree. They'll tell you about getting your name out there and hoping something sticks. But, this is not REAL marketing.

There are so many ways to be smart about growing your tax business. Having Direct Response Marketing as your foundation is best if you are the owner of a small-to-medium size business. The same is true for large companies. But they are using other people's money while trying to impress their board members. (This is not the place for me to explain the numerous marketing agendas of large companies.) Anyway, Direct Marketing strategies are THE place to hang your hat and focus your attention if you're serious about growing your tax practice with a nice Return On Investment (ROI).

Direct Marketing (I use Direct Response Marketing interchangeably here as well) has been interwoven into the fabric of successful, growing businesses for over a hundred years. It's measurable. It's accountable. And when used properly, it works!

Note: Everything I'll be sharing with you in this advanced section will have Direct Response Marketing as its foundation.

Now, let's get into some of the CHANGES that are best for taking your tax business to the next level of success.

CHANGE WHERE YOU SELL

You can change the media you advertise in. Think of media as the platform for your marketing message. Just make a list where you advertise now. Where have you advertised in the past? What worked and what didn't work so well? Do you even know for sure? (Hint: When you use Direct Response Marketing, you are much more likely to be able to quantify the results.)

If your tax business advertising results have not been stellar in the past, I wouldn't recommend blaming it on the media you used. In my experience, the media usually isn't the problem. In most cases, **when a tax business promotion loses money or doesn't work like you hoped, it's usually a TARGET MARKET or MESSAGE problem.**

But let's say you do have an ad that's working for you. The promotion is bringing you an acceptable ROI, so what do you do next?

You might be surprised, but by just taking that same ad which is already working for you and running the promotion in other media, you can double or triple your results. In many cases, you barely have to change your ad. All you have done is leverage your marketing message and added it to a few more platforms (MEDIA). The right media gets the attention of your target market and when run in tandem with other promotions, momentum occurs. This multi-media effect actually provides an extra boost to all of your campaigns when compared to just running a stand-alone promotion.

CHANGE WHO IS SELLING

Another way to boost your tax business promotional results is to change WHO is doing the selling.

You can change who in your office is allowed to speak with prospects and who is best to speak with existing clients. In our tax business, only a few key people were selected to speak with a prospect over the phone or if they walked in our office. (We treated an opportunity to gain a new client like gold.) Having a high-priority mentality inside the office, that selling an appointment or getting someone new to come in and give us a try, was critically important to our success.

This mentality is important for an OUTSIDE sales team, too.

Did you realize your existing tax clients are THE best sales team you have for spreading the "good news" about your tax business? Go out of your way to treat them like your secret agent sales force. Be purposeful about gathering your top ten or twelve "best referring" clients. They love talking about you and your tax business anyway.

Pick a date and invite your "champion" clients to come together with you at the same time. Feed them and give away a few nice gifts, showing appreciation for being some of your "Top Referring" Clients. Look them in the eyes and tell them what a difference they make in your life! Then give them permission to take your Refer-A-Friend Program and run with it to the next level. Offer additional "sales material" for these word-of-mouth experts to pass along to their co-workers, neighbors and family members.

Obviously, if you can incentivize them even further, do so as you see fit. If your state's law or your professional license would not approve, no problem, just tell them you love them with hand-written thank you notes. (Many times hand-written thank you notes work better than money!)

ANOTHER KIND OF OUTSIDE SALES TEAM

As you know, there are already boatloads of sales people on the streets calling on small business owners to buy various products and services. Why not add a couple of them to sell for you?

Seek out insurance agents, mortgage brokers, financial service reps or other sales people not necessarily representing the tax-related industry. As long as they spend most of their time getting in front of small business owners (even well-matched taxpayers without a small business) and selling something, you can SELL THEM on generating leads for you!

Here's what I mean. If a sales person is going to be in front of a potential client who might need tax help anyway, is it that big of a deal to inquire about the prospect's tax situation? The sales person should be asking a lot of qualifying questions anyway. Bringing up how satisfied they are with their current tax professional is not hard.

If tax problems do come up in the conversation or if there's any interest at all in looking at another tax pro option, the sales person can hand them a pre-prepared packet explaining your tax business, including your core sales message, main story and testimonials from other small business owners.

This takes sixty seconds of a sales person's time and you get a qualified lead WITHOUT paying in promotional dollars up front for the inquiry. If the prospect turns into a client, your sales person gets paid a finder's fee. This is a win/win for everyone!

CHANGE LOCATION: OUT OF CATEGORY

This is one of my favorite "out-of-the-box" leads-generating and selling strategies for a tax practice. Go someplace where thousands of quality prospects congregate. Make sure no other tax professional in your area will go there. And – by the way – these potential tax clients will have already predetermined in their minds the need to buy something.

Where am I talking about? *The Home & Garden Expo*. There's one of these three day events in your area every spring (usually March). The businesses who buy a booth are mostly home and garden-related vendors. The people who pay to walk around and look at all the vendor's booths are home-owners and/or folks with extra disposable income.

Are your competitors there? No way -- they are buried in their offices doing tax returns. So guess what? When you get a booth, not only are you the ONLY tax business in the whole Expo, but you get to answer tax questions from quality middle-to-higher income home-owners.

Let me just tell you from experience in working these kinds of Expos, YOU GET TONS OF QUALITY LEADS and in some cases you can set appointments right on the spot.

You'll want to man the booth with an outgoing person who likes to talk to people (qualify, gather leads) and an experienced tax preparer (offering nuggets of free advice, but mostly scheduling follow-up appointments back in your office.)

Because you are talking to good prospects who are seeking out vendors to spend money with, and it's happening right in the middle of tax season, the three days out of your office is time very well spent.

ANOTHER OUT OF CATEGORY LOCATION

Your local County Fair. Our tax business started getting a booth in August at the County Fair to help sell our tax schools, which we taught beginning in September. Little did we know, but the people who visited our booth weren't interested in preparing their own taxes. They wanted to speak to someone about filing their taxes.

Again, we had no competition.

All the vendors were Farm and Food related. Turns out we picked up a ton of back-work from years of folks not filing returns. And it wasn't just taxpayers, but many really good small business clients found us initially at the Fair, on a dirt floor, right next to the cows!

CHANGE WHO YOU SELL TO

First, let me be clear. Savvy tax pros always look to sell to other quality clients similar to the ones already in their client database. They find small segments of clients grouped together in their list who have proved to be excellent people to work with. OBVIOUSLY, YOUR FIRST PRIORITY IS TO SELL TO THESE KINDS OF FOLKS FIRST.

Then, I want you to block off some time to brainstorm with a couple of friends or family members and begin to remind yourself about your existing **relationship capital**. You might not realize it, but you have RELATIONSHIP ASSETS buried in your tax business, too. These relationships are with people who can bring great value to your tax practice. Like lost treasure, if you knew where the gold was buried, wouldn't you try and dig it up?

Note: Please don't over-complicate what I'm about to say. (The reason I'm bringing up this simple strategy is, historically, tax pros are terrible at basic networking.) You can make a list of all the people you know in your city today. They don't have to be hugely influential. But it helps if they have a group of folks in their personal circle of influence to be able to spread the word about your tax business.

What makes networking work well is having a great HOOK. This is an attention-getting reason why taxpayers should seriously consider you verse all the other tax filing options available to them. Sound familiar? You can compile a separate Unique Selling Proposition for your tax business just for networking purposes.

Low-Hanging Fruit Strategy

Contact your existing business owner tax clients or leaders in the community who have access to a nice size list if your relationship with them is so good that they will endorse you to others at the drop of a hat.

Another segment of your tax clients won't have big lists to endorse you to, but they know other people who do. They can easily make an introduction for you. The key is WHAT'S IN IT FOR THEM? (The answer to this will be one of your USP's.)

CHANGE WHY THEY COME TO YOU

When you go fishing, you better have some good bait. Because if the fish aren't biting, you'll be just wasting your time throwing your line into the water. Same is true when tax businesses invest their hard-earned money advertising their services.

Some of the best "bait" I know of is a book with your name and picture on it. A book positions you as an expert attracting the "quality fish" your tax business most wants to catch.

Being a tax professional with a book is powerful. Better yet, promoting your book with the right kind of marketing will actually open up many more doors for you to highlight your tax services to the target market you most want as clients.

The problem is you don't have the time or even want to write a book. You might not think you're a good enough writer or that you could ever complete a project like actually writing a book. The truth is you really could do it if you wanted to. You're already an expert on the tax related topics you'd cover. It's just a matter of getting words on paper.

In the real world, most book authors hire someone else to write the book for them. Or a business owner will pay for a book license and get their name, picture and contact info added to a specialized book already written. This kind of book license gives them permission to use the book as a promotional tool to promote their business.

Which is really the only reason you want the book anyway:

Bait.

Here's a practice example of this strategy.

www.MillionDollarTaxBiz.com/ACABook

Local Celebrity Status

Another big reason why taxpayers will call you verses your competition is that they have seen, heard, or read about you in the local media. Once you've been interviewed or the media asks you to comment on tax- related issues in the news, your credibility factor skyrockets.

Once a TV station, radio personality, newspaper reporter or even community activist with a popular blog features you on their media platform, the halo effect comes into play and you are now anointed with "expert status" for all the taxpayers in your market area to witness.

But here's the interesting part. Getting free publicity (interviews with the media) is NOT that hard to do. If you follow through on a few simple steps, you can achieve a higher level of local status in your community and most importantly, CREATE ANOTHER REASON WHY TAXPAYERS SHOULD CONTACT YOU FOR TAX HELP.

When you send out a press release, your goal is not to get a small write-up in the local paper. The goal of your press release is to land an interview. That means the press release is completely different than what you might have sent to the media in the past. Accompanying your attention-grabbing press release is your list of provocative questions. If answered, these questions make a great story and the media knows it.

That's truly what the media wants: a Great Story. And since tax-related issues are constantly in the news during tax season, you can BE the local angle they are looking to interview. (Just give the media what they want and you'll get everything you want for your tax business.)

Speaking of interviews, have you ever considered being the interviewer?

Another sneaky little trick few tax pros in our industry ever consider doing is interviewing the most influential people in your city. Why would you do this? Because when you're seen connecting with the movers and shakers in your local area, state or region, your status as a professional rises.

You have your own media to your clients whether you realize it or not. Your monthly newsletter is media. Your weekly email updates are media. Even videos you post on your online social network help build your platform for being an authority in the area of taxes. This platform gives you an excuse to contact top leaders in your city, the mayor, heads of corporations – even celebrities -- and ask them their views on various issues.

You'll be surprised at how many people say yes because they love having their ego stroked.

No other tax pros in your area will do this. This strategy sets you apart and adds more reasons why people will talk about you. And during tax season, your word-of-mouth referrals will spread like wildfire.

So these are examples of ways to reinvent your tax business. Changing WHERE you sell, WHO you sell to and WHY they come to you turns the table on your competition, giving you an "unfair" advantage promoting your practice.

The Leap Frog Strategy

I'd like to go deeper with a few of the advanced marketing strategies we just discussed. To do this, I'll explain them in the context of what I call The Leap Frog Strategy.

BLOCKBUSTER
How To Build A Million Dollar Tax Business

The Leap Frog concept is very appealing because no matter where you are on the tax business ladder of success, you can breakthrough and 'leap' to the top and be the most successful tax practitioner in your area. No waiting in line or paying your dues.

I recommend completely changing the category so your tax business is THE option when your marketing campaign hits the streets. You can decide to be the niche leader in a particular category because you say so.

You don't have to get permission from someone else. If you want to focus on The Affordable Care Act, your advertising can acknowledge you as THE leading healthcare tax professional in your city. You could be the top CPA in your city specializing in helping teachers file their taxes. No other tax pros in your market area are singling out teachers as their core target group they service. In this example, you would be the leader in this category.

This is an example of the Leap Frog Strategy. You define the terms. You pick a niche group to serve where you automatically win. You are either the only tax pro with this positioning or you are so good at helping a particular targeted group in a geographic area that no one can knock you off your throne.

After you establish your territory, it's time to build a fence around your herd to keep any poachers from stealing the taxpayers you've marked as best tax clients for you.

You can control the media. You should have your own newsletter both online and offline. The topics will include your expert analysis on the issues your niche target market most wants info on. And, of course, you'll add interviews with your best clients sharing glowing testimonials about you and your tax business. Many of these interviews work best when used in multiple formats.

Another example of a format to use is a *Video Magazine.* Videos are even easier to record (just pull that smart phone out of your pocket). You can easily shoot two- or three-minute videos – "man on the street" style – covering different interesting topics. You can also post these same videos on various kinds of social media as lead generators. They will promote your Video Magazine and extend your reach even more so you'll dominate the category of your choice.

Don't forget, you can host your own webinar and teleseminars. They're easy to do. They're very inexpensive, and they help you leverage your message to your target audience. When the movers and shakers in your niche category see you hosting these kinds of platforms for your clients, some will try to seek you out and then more opportunities will come your way. All of this expert positioning piles up and makes you the leader in your niche.

Note: You can serve multiple niche markets AT THE SAME TIME. Don't limit yourself. It's actually best to leverage the work you are doing in one category, change a few words around and roll out 90 percent of the same material in the next niche category. This is how wealth becomes systemized so you end up working less and making more.

Once you master this, you'll actually become your own local celebrity. You'll be asked to attend insider lunches representing the business sector in your city.

The media will contact you more often when they need a story on taxes. You'll start to receive invitations to participate in charity fund-raising events.

(Hint: Start your own charity now, because if you go to theirs, they'll come to yours. Plus these charity events provide excellent set-ups for future endorsement opportunities for your tax business.)

You'll be known as "THE tax pro in _____" because of the high profile you've established. Your newsletters, webinars and videos will go viral on Facebook, Twitter and all the other online social media. By being purposeful in these areas I've described, you WILL leap over every other tax business in your area.

Here's some more good news.

The majority of your tax business competitors will NOT do what I just said. And guess what? That's why only five percent of the tax pros in the country are truly successful at running their tax business. And since your competition is going to keep doing what they've always done, it's time for you to get busy and start Leap Frogging!

You're going to be more successful taking this renegade approach. Advanced marketing is NOT doing the same old stuff. But the reward for the extra work is more revenue, more clients and more freedom to live life on your own terms.

Chapter 6

"Work Less ... Make More" Tax Biz Profit Strategies

"Work Less, Make More!" It's what every tax business owner wants, but most believe it will never happen to them. They think it's a pipe dream. They think it's not reality. Well, I'm here to tell you, that you can make this four-word phrase a reality in your life. If you have the guts to do what I tell you to do, you'll see a significant shift in your tax business and you WILL work less and make more money.

Most tax professionals think of their clients one-by-one. One client, then another client, etc. Meaning, you treat all your clients the same. If you have 100 clients or you have 1,000 clients, by most accounts, they all get equal treatment, right?

The truth is, they shouldn't. Usually tax business owners spend approximately the same amount of time and resources and deliver the same follow-up communication with each client. That's NOT a good idea.

Why?

Because every client listed in your database has an UNEQUAL capacity, desire or even tax filing status for paying you more for your time and expertise. In addition, your clients will buy even more of your products and services, plus many other professional services you endorse, if you encourage them.

Treating all of your clients the same doesn't make any sense. Allow your clients to make their own choices. They will tell you what they want by the money they give you when they buy more. The problem with most tax pros is they rarely sift and sort their client list with multiple offers on a year-round basis. So if you're only making one offer, one time of year (tax preparation) I guess everyone on your list does look the same.

Go back to The 80/20 Rule. Tax pros understand the concept, but don't apply it to their business in a practical way.

Remember ...

Eighty percent of your profit comes from 20 percent of your clients. Eighty percent of your stress, problems and headaches come from about 20 percent of your clients. The new clients who contact your office usually come from about 20 percent of your ads. If you have five employees, you and I both know that one of them stands out head and shoulders above the rest. (That's one out of five or 20 percent.)

Let's talk time. In your typical ten-hour work day, chances are high there's about two hours in there where you're most productive and the other eight hours are not as much. Again, this is all 80/20.

Now, I'm just broad stroking this concept AGAIN because I want you to understand where I'm coming from. Leveraging the power of The 80/20 Rule MUST happen with your clients if you truly want to work less and make more money.

As the owner, you've got to make some decisions. Which clients are you going to spend more of your time with? Which clients are most likely to pay you more, offering the highest margins? What products or services will you invest your time and effort into? What brings the greatest return when you get personally involved? What can you do to make your employees most effective?

And lastly, WHAT OFFICE TASKS, TAX SERVICES OR GENERAL BUSINESS DUTIES DO YOU NEED TO QUIT DOING ASAP IN ORDER TO BE INVOLVED IN MORE PRODUCTIVE PRIORITIES FOR YOUR TAX PRACTICE? (This includes figuring out what existing clients you need to pass along for someone else in your office to handle.)

Let's look at your schedule. What projects are you working on? What kind of workload is normally on your plate? Are you mostly working IN your business or do you have consistent, large chunks of time where you work ON your business?

Okay, here's the Million Dollar Question:

About those projects, tasks and whatever you're working on, however you're doing it .... Are they bringing you closer to your tax business' goals or not?

I can tell you from many years of consulting and coaching tax business owners, they might set some goals, but tax pros rarely attach their time and task list for the current week to a specific, measured goal months or years away.

You might have some target goals you say are important to you, but how you spend your time and money leading up to those goals are different. Does where you invest your time and where you focus your energy match with reaching your stated goals?

Usually they don't. So this lack of continuity obviously affects why you don't get to where you say you want to go in your business.

But there is a simple fix to this problem.

Just shift where you spend your time and energy so your efforts DO align with your goals. If you get this realization and adjust your daily and weekly schedule accordingly, half the battle is already won!

If you shoot for 80 percent of your projects aligning with your actual stated goals, you will be remarkably effective at attracting much more success to your business and your life. Now in the real world, you can't expect 100-percent compliance. Stuff happens. But keep in mind: this is just another way 80/20 is in play.

Dirty Little Marketing Secret

Most tax pros don't know this, **but really good marketing actually REPELS 80 percent of the people who see the ad and ATTRACTS like a magnet the other 20 percent.**

So how are you at qualifying your prospects? Talking to better quality taxpayers more likely to love what your tax business does saves a ton of time. And when they actually become a client, you'll make even more money dealing with them.

I really want you to get the fact that purposefully disqualifying many of the people right out of the gate, when they are exposed to your promotion, is a very effective workless, make-more technique. You should NOT say "yes" to every person that calls your office to do business. You actually need to qualify them. Do they have money? Or do they seem like they are only interested in a lowball price?

Is there some sense of urgency? Is their tax situation bringing them pain? Or is there some kind of significant loss or major inconvenience on the horizon you can help them with? Or can you tell if gaining pleasure is on their mind? Maybe there is a significant tax refund sitting right there in front of them. Does this impact their interest in handling their tax situation quickly or not? If you don't sense a spring in their step when telling them you are able to help give them what they want, they may not be a good prospect for you to do business with.

Do they buy into your Unique Selling Proposition? This is the main reason why people choose you versus other tax filing options available to them. Basically, you want to know if they really want what your tax practice is offering. If they're hesitant on the phone, it's okay. You don't have to say yes to them. You don't have to "hard sell" them on coming into your office either. Sometimes reverse psychology is best. Play hard to get. Even turn them loose and encourage them to call your competition because you are confident no one else helps taxpayers in the area like your tax practice does. If they call you back, they will be a quality client.

*One Last Heads Up To You About
Your Client List*

In EVERY list, there's always a WHALE. That means **there's at least one person in your database capable and willing, under the right circumstances and with the right offer, to spend a VERY LARGE AMOUNT OF MONEY with your tax business.** In some cases, this one client could boost your tax firm's overall NET PROFIT by as much as 25-to-50 percent!

Let me give you an example. I know of a small seasonal tax preparation practice with 250 clients. The owner was grossing about $100,000 in annual revenue. After a meeting with one of his clients, he landed a monthly account worth $25,000 annually. Turns out, the revenue from this one client ended up being 20 percent of his net income. Needless to say, this tax practitioner began targeting other similar small businesses. Now his core business is finding well-matched clients who are willing and able to do the same. He hires out most of the day-to-day work. So today this tax pro makes more than he ever did and works fewer hours than ever before.

Tax Business Owner Productivity

We all like to be efficient. We all like to be productive. The question is, are we being productive on the right stuff? How do you prioritize your day? What does a normal work day look like for you? Do you time block? Do you assign a certain number of minutes or hours to certain projects? Do you do first things first, the most important items on your list? Do you have clarity on what IS most important to do in your business? Are you clear about what you're NOT to touch or get involved in with respect to operating your business? Do you know what to look for, so when the right opportunity presents itself to you, you can take advantage?

Way too often, tax business owners have NO clear path. They're not sure what they should be working on to make a significant jump to the next level. Business as usual is par for the course. You might be a big checklist person. Let's say there are 20 items on the to-do list for the day. In order to make you, the checklist tax pro, feel good, you will start doing stuff on the list that takes two or three minutes here, five minutes there or only 15 minutes, etc. The morning hours are gone and 17 items on the list are completed. You, the owner, feel good about yourself. Then you take a lunch break, come back to the office, and the top three most important items on the list have not been touched. Now it's the afternoon, you feel sluggish and tend to be distracted more. Do you finish any of these higher priority tasks? Not really.

The next day, a similar schedule happens. You "accomplish" the easy-to-check-off-the-list stuff first, while handling the incoming calls and emails of the day. You have lunch and get back to your office for the high priority tasks. But, of course, a problem arises. Then more issues come onto your plate because your staff keeps interrupting you. Your afternoon is done. You finish the day. You go home. You accomplished some work. You were able to cross out 15 or 16 items of the 20 on your list. However, what about the status of those "important" projects?

You see, the really critical projects which are key to making your tax business more successful usually can't be accomplished in an afternoon. Plus, since you are the owner, no one is breathing down your neck wanting these kinds of business priorities completed. You know they are important. But your employees don't really care that much because it's not their business. So the "important stuff" gets delayed or pushed off to another time until it's too late. Now tax season is here and you don't have time to implement what you know would be best for the business. Sound familiar?

The LIE is you feel like you're being productive. But in the real world, this deception is keeping you from success.

So then the question comes up, "Well, what if I can never get to those 15, 16, 17 things?" First of all, they're probably not that important, so it would be ok. Secondly, this is why you have a team. Even one part-time employee's job could be completing the 10 to 15 items that come up on the owner's list each day. (That's it.) It's called delegate the small stuff so the owner makes time for the real business-growth stuff.

For small tax offices, the response I get is, "I don't have someone I trust to delegate these lower level tasks to." That's hogwash, but let me give you a solution even though the premise is wrong. Time-block these lower level tasks to be worked on between three and five o'clock p.m. only. You free up your most productive hours in your day for what's most important. And if two hours in the afternoon isn't enough, they will have to wait until the next afternoon. Truth be told, when you limit yourself to only a short time frame, these kinds of tasks tend to be completed faster.

The same time-blocking principle applies here, too. Decide what your most productive times during your work week are and give your best energy to these priority projects. (Example: Tuesdays and Thursday's from 10 a.m. to 1 p.m., plus Wednesdays from 9 a.m. to 12 noon). If you commit to no interruptions during these high-payoff productivity time slots, you will be well on your way to growing your tax business extremely effectively.

Technology and Information Overload

Problems tend to arise when we gain clarity about our priorities but then can't seem to make time to complete tasks related to these priorities. Often the culprit is too much technology and information overload. For every tax business owner, these potential time-sucking vampires can be a blessing or a curse.

Are you the master or the slave with regards to emails, texts, social media and phone calls? Technology and access to new information these days really can be overwhelming, if you let it. To accomplish anything of substance, you're going to have to say no to more information and technology. Say yes to taking no phone calls, keeping your email account closed and turning off your mobile phone for several hours in a row, multiple times during your day. I promise, this won't kill you!

Addicted ...
Don't Let This Happen To You

I told this guy at one of my Tax Business Success Events to unsubscribe to emails that were not making him money. His tax business was drowning. He was just overwhelmed. He was the definition of information overload. This guy looked at me with a weird face when I said to stop wasting time on emails so he could run his business properly. Then I asked him how much time he spent per day on emails. He told me, "I spend five to six hours a day just reading my email," and I looked at him and I said, "Reading what kind of email?" He said, "Well, I subscribe to a lot of different things and I'm just reading everybody's stuff and sometimes I respond to it, but mostly I'm just reading information, keeping up-to-date and being informed." I thought to myself, "The guy's business is going in the toilet and he's spending 25 to 30 hours of his week reading email?"

At the end of the seminar we were doing Hot Seats. (This is when I offer advice to tax biz owners in front of everyone else in the room.) When we got to this guy's turn, he had a big long list of all these different strategies he wanted to use from what he just learned at my event. I stopped him before he could get to the end of his to-do list and said, "Actually you shouldn't do any of those strategies. I want you to do one thing. Cancel your current email address and get a new email. Give the new email address to your clients, family and friends. And don't give your email out to anyone else for a minimum of one year."

Then I proclaimed, "You just gained (at least) five hours a day for the next year – and no more burden of reading other people's info. How does that feel?"

He looked at me and said, "I can't do that." I said, "Why not?" He replied, "I just can't do it. That's my life. That's what I do." The guy was addicted to reading these emails. I felt so sorry for him because he couldn't turn them off.

Are You A Master Or Slave To Money?

Our goal is to work less and make more money. Taming the technology tiger is part of the answer. Gaining extra time in your schedule is very valuable, too. (Even if your situation is not as extreme as my live event attendee we just discussed.) But what about money itself?

How do you view money? Money is not good or evil. However, when you accept certain clients, the money they give you comes with its own price.

So let me ask you, "Are you a master or a slave to money?"

Sometimes you have to say no to a lucrative financial deal because it runs contrary to what you believe is right. Another reason you would say no to a good solid money deal would be the project doesn't get you closer to the stated goals of your business. Maybe a new client wants to hire you for a service, but it's not the best use of your time. Maybe the profit margins are not in line because you would need to personally babysit the project.

IF YOU SAY YES TO ANY KIND CLIENT WANTING YOU TO DO WHATEVER TYPE OF SERVICE JUST TO GET PAID ….

YOU ARE A SLAVE TO MONEY.

BLOCKBUSTER
How To Build A Million Dollar Tax Business

Are you the boss of how you make your money? Are you the boss of how you spend your time? Are you the decision maker for how you prioritize your day?

Be the MASTER of your money. Don't let trying to make a buck dictate your life.

Giving yourself the freedom to say no is powerful. What will I cross off my list? What am I going to delegate? What services am I going to stop offering immediately, especially those that don't turn a profit or have low margins?

You might be thinking, "What am I going to do with all this extra time on my hands?"

Well, one of the strategies I learned early on growing our tax business to the multi-million dollar level was profoundly simple, but a very effective use of my time.

Every day I took the time to sit down in a quiet place, with pen and paper in hand and ...

THINK.

No specific projects in mind, no computers or phones, no news or sports -- everything off and silent.

Try it. You'll be blown away by the clarity you get about your life.

One hour a day, five days a week.

This THINKING time will change your business forever.

Eliminating Your Hate List

Every tax business owner has a Hate List. This is all the stuff you deal with each week or month because you feel like it just comes with the territory of being The Boss. What if you didn't have to do these things? Better yet, how many opportunities for growing your tax business come up but are not even considered because some part of the process involves something you "hate" doing?

Let me ask this question a different way: What new ideas for your tax business have you resisted in the past because you assumed you had to figure out how everything worked first? Or you believed everything had to run through you because you're the owner?

Translation: Because you believed owners must be at the center of important projects.

Do you believe that you're the only one in your office capable of doing high priority projects? If you're not sure, just look at the projects you're taking on now or on a regular basis. What I'm trying to get across to you is this:

YOU DON'T ALWAYS HAVE TO BE THE ONE WHO IS IN CHARGE OF TAKING ON NEW PROJECTS.

So many tax professionals feel like they must have a complete understanding of whatever it is before they feel comfortable moving forward on a project. Talk about stunting your growth potential. Many tax pros won't take on ideas that are best for their business because they personally don't want to deal with it. This is small-time thinking. Just because the owner can't have their fingers in it, doesn't mean a new successful strategy shouldn't get implemented.

If this is you, either there's a fear of delegation or you're afraid to outsource. Maybe you got burned a little in the past from your employees not following through on an initiative. However, if you continue on this same path, the growth ceiling above your head is not going to move very much. And you'll be stuck.

Let's revisit this delegation issue real quick, but in the context of getting rid of the unwanted tasks on your hate list.

Circle of Commitment

There is a Circle of Commitment that happens when you properly delegate.

You have a project needing to be completed in your office. You choose an employee and make a request for them to handle it. Since you are their employer, they listen to what you want them to do. After a back-and-forth dialogue to clarify what this completed project would look like, you come to an agreement on timing. The employee has other priorities on their plate and can't do what you asked by Friday, but they do ask if next Tuesday would work. This is the negotiation portion of the Circle of Commitment. You could have said, "No, I've got to have this done by Friday." And as The Boss, you would give permission to stop work on the current projects so this new project could get moved to the head of the line.

Before you leave, you both are clear (in writing) about what needs to happen for this project to be considered successful. But what about the "stuff" that sometimes happens between now and the completion date? When delegating, always include a scheduled check-in time somewhere in the middle of the project. This will allow you the chance to review the work and make sure it's on track to meet your expectations. By the same token, this check-in time slot provides a safe opportunity for your employee to ask follow up questions so they don't feel like they're bugging you during your busy day.

This is a healthy delegation process.

Sad to say, dumping (not delegating) is what normally happens in the tax industry. You're busy. "Hey, Joe, take this project. I need it by Thursday. I'll talk to you later." Joe gets it done (mostly), but not exactly like you want. The truth is, you did a poor job giving Joe all the information he needed to complete the project properly. Or maybe Joe didn't hear you well because the specifics were never in writing. Either way, Joe got dumped on, and as a result the flow in your tax office hit a few bumps.

Because this kind of miscommunication happens too much in your office, you say, "Forget delegation. I'll just do it myself."

That's not the best way to grow a successful tax business. And, of course, you'll never work less and make more money going this route.

What's On Your Love List?

What energizes you? What do you love to do when running your tax business?

Three or four activities usually generate the most wealth for a tax business. Are you good at any of those things? Prospecting for well-matched tax clients for your business? Converting quality prospects to paying, high-margin clients? What about negotiating the sale of other tax practices and growing through acquisition? Are you exceptional at meeting with potential clients and helping them feel great about using your services? Are you a top shelf trainer who really enjoys hiring staff and getting them comfortable with your tax office operational system?

My guess is you probably love to serve people and help them solve their tax problems so they're able to file an accurate return to Uncle Sam.

But here's the rub.

If you are the owner, preparing tax returns (even if you love to do them) is a poor use of your time. I know you got into this business to do tax returns. But if you want to take your tax business to the million dollar level, you must begin transitioning a large portion of your tax clients to other tax preparers in your office.

Work Only Two Hours A Day?

What if you only had two hours a day to work? You couldn't work any more hours than two per day. What would you work on? What would you delegate immediately? Would you spend your time doing taxes or would you invest your time into others in your office?

How would you train your staff on one day and then check up on them the next day? Would you provide additional resources and success tools so everyone in the office could access them while you were not available?

Well, in my opinion, you should actually DO THIS for a month. If you force yourself to only go into your office for two hours a day and not allow any phone calls, emails or texts from your staff until right before you see them the following day, what do you think would happen?

TRANSFORMATION.

In one month, your tax business and your life will be changed for life. You will NOT go back to the old way – I promise!

<u>Don't hear me say after the two hours, I think you should take the rest of the day off. No, the two hours per day at your office is an investment in your employees.</u> **The other hours in the day need to be an investment in YOU.**

You need to sharpen the sword mentally, physically, spiritually and professionally. You must allow yourself time to work on things you know you need to get better at in order to lead your business to the next level.

Some tax professionals tell me they have to be first in and last to leave their office. That's baloney, just "baggage from your past" thoughts poisoning your mind.

Working that many hours might make you feel good about yourself in the short run. But if you continue that mentality, you're never going to work less and make more money.

Acres of Diamonds

Now, let me leave you with one final nugget to help you work less and make more.

If you have never read the book *Acres of Diamonds*, go to Amazon and buy it now. (Read it once you finish this book.) Here's the punchline: There's money right under your nose in your client list; increase your profits inside your current list first before spending a bunch of time and energy trying to make more money in other places.

Well, everyone gets the wisdom of that advice. But the next question in their brain is, "How do I do that?"

You start by data mining your own client list. Get a profile of your best clients by answering these three simple questions:

How *frequently* do your clients come in?

How *recently* have your clients contacted you?

How much *money* do your clients spend with you?

Track your answers to these three questions. Everyone does this differently, so decide what parameters are best for your tax business and go with them. Once you've compiled this data, you'll see patterns emerge.

Pay attention to ….

Who do you NET the most profit from?

(Separate seasonal tax prep vs. year-round tax-related services?)

What year does a client need to hit to be considered a lifer?

(Example: If a client sticks with you for five years, are they likely to stay decades?)

How many trends or similarities can you spot in your client list?

(Certain kinds of occupations or geographic locations or demographics?)

BLOCKBUSTER
How To Build A Million Dollar Tax Business

If you've never taken your database through this process before, you'll be THRILLED at what you learn about your best clients. This will be the beginning of YOUR acres of diamonds!

All of a sudden, your priorities as the owner will change. You'll see the advantages of working smarter, not harder, right in front of you. Based on what you discover from your deep-dive into your client list, you'll want to focus your time and attention on attaining more of these "best" clients.

Remember, birds of a feather flock together.

Ask your best clients ...

What organizations do they belong to?

Where do they spend their time when not at work?

What media do they watch, read or listen to?

In very little time, your marketing plan will attain laser-like focus. Because you now know exactly the type of client best matched for your tax practice, you won't waste tons of time and money promoting your business in other places to other people.

From a marketing perspective, this is how to work less and make more -- a lot more!

Overall, I covered a lot of ground in this chapter. But truthfully, this whole book is about working less and making more. So keep reading. I've got a much more to share with you.

You truly can do this.

You WILL take your tax business to the next level!

Chapter 7

Increasing Your Tax Biz's #1 Source for New Clients

Without a doubt, when you survey the tax industry, tax business owners will tell you: referrals are the number one source for new clients. And I say, "Of course referrals are your number one source for new clients. You are in the SERVICE business!" When you're in a service business, you better have clients telling others about you because if you don't, your "service" is probably pretty stale.

Helping someone file their taxes is a very personal thing. You have a snapshot of their life right in front of you. So if you're really good at your craft (helping people file their taxes well) and you show plenty of empathy for your client's financial situation, then you'll get plenty of additional word-of-mouth business.

Now paying attention to referrals is obviously a big deal. Referrals can be (and should be) the life blood of your tax business. But for some tax pros, referrals are the ONLY new clients they get.

Why just referrals?

Many times tax professionals will put together a promotion for their business. The campaign gets poor results or the ad they run doesn't get much response. That means the tax business owner just spent some of their hard-earned money on marketing and didn't see any financial return for their efforts. So then, they'll throw their hands up and say, "Forget it. I'm not doing that anymore. I seem to get my best new clients from existing clients telling other people about me anyway. So I guess I'll just grow my tax business that way."

Now trying to grow your tax practice by referral only is good, but very slow. Of course, it's a much faster process when you have MANY "marketing irons" in the fire spreading the word about you and your business.

Benefits From Referred Clients

When you land a few new client referrals, remember that the endorsement you get from one of your existing clients brings many added benefits. The new client coming into your office is easier to work with. They are pre-disposed to follow whatever advice you give them. And don't forget, a new referred client has much less price resistance than a taxpayer who saw your sign driving down the road and decided to pull in and check you out. Overall, pre-sold referrals are better for reducing your stress and increasing the size of your wallet.

Another huge advantage tax business owners often don't realize: A referred client is already trained to refer others. (This is BIG.) Remember, being a referral was their entry point for coming to work with you. Properly trained (and you do have to train everyone who does business with you), a new client like this can become a referral machine.

Don't think huge referral numbers just happen randomly. They can on rare occasions. But for the most part, **a tax pro running their successful service business will have a clear vision for gathering other like-minded clients through**

word-of-mouth marketing. This vision can be broken down into manageable and measureable action steps. So when you have a clarified, purposed plan divided into bite-sized strategies, with everyone in your office on the same page, your clients will understand the process much easier and refer even more new clients than you ever thought possible.

Where To Start

How do you set the tone as the tax business owner? How do you begin the process of making your tax business become characterized as a well-oiled, word-of-mouth, referral machine in your community, city or even region?

Well, the number one place to start comes from building a foundation. This foundation is a culture in your office – a referral culture.

Referrals permeate everything you do. You discuss them in meetings. Referrals come up in conversations with your employees. Your year-round staff naturally passes your priority for word-of-mouth business along to seasonal tax preparers during tax season. Referrals ring clear in all of your client communications. "This is what we do here." A successful client in our office always finds other people like themselves and encourages them to come to our tax office.

When you send letters to your clients or you have email correspondences, there's a consistent drumbeat of talk about referrals: How you appreciate them and how you go out of your way to take care of the friends, family and co-workers your clients send to your tax practice.

BLOCKBUSTER
How To Build A Million Dollar Tax Business

"Spread The Word" Office Environment

When you walk into your tax office, is it stale like most other tax or accounting offices? Or does the environment purposefully build a bond with the people who come into your work space? Is it evident that people are taking the word to their friends? Does the newcomer see successful clients spreading the word about your tax business and then, as a result, realize that their friends will soon take part in your office's tax filing multiplier effect?

You may have posters on your lobby wall promoting your Refer-A-Friend program. Or pictures featuring testimonials of your clients talking about how great your tax services are and how easy it is to participate in the Refer-A-Friend Program. (Or whatever you call your referral program. It's important for your Referral Program to have a name.)

One of our most effective signs ever was placed on the wall of each cubicle in our tax offices. Each of our tax offices was a high-volume, fast-paced environment. Clients walked in (most did not make appointments) and had their taxes done that same day while sitting with a tax preparer. As our employee sat across the desk from the client, preparing the return, the client couldn't help seeing the sign we had strategically positioned on the wall of the tax-preparing station, right over the employee's shoulder.

The sign was a Simple Referral Outline (a 1, 2, 3 Step Process) which encouraged our clients to begin thinking about their friends, family members and even the coworkers they could encourage to have their taxes filed with us.

Through the signage, we were teaching them how best to refer others before their tax service was even finished! This orientation was part of the referral culture of our tax business.

BLOCKBUSTER
How To Build A Million Dollar Tax Business

We made it clear we wanted all of our clients to be thrilled with their service, and we wanted them to tell the world (their circle of influence at home, in their neighborhood or at work) what we were all about because of it.

What About Referral Incentives?

The question always comes up: Do you compensate your clients for referrals? The answer is YES and NO. I'm going to give you the pros and cons for both because both ways (whether you pay for referrals or not) are okay.

If you want to financially reward your clients for bringing your new clients – great. But if you don't (or you can't because of your professional license or state regulation), it's still okay. You can go about it both ways and have a thriving referral practice.

In our tax business, we did both.

If somebody came in to get their taxes done and said, "Joe told me about you guys and I'm here," then we would say, "Great, thank you. Have a seat." But if that same guy walked in an hour earlier and said, "Joe told me to come get my taxes done here and this is my refer-a-friend slip," ... well, we measure those new RAF clients and financially reward both parties. When one of these RAF slips was handed to the tax preparer, we captured a name and the last four digits of their social security number at the bottom of that slip. We tracked the referral back to the person who did the referring so we could reward them. In our case, we gave them cash!

We offered a small token of appreciation, anywhere from $10 to $20. And after years of testing, we found that $10 in cash was more effective when we did this one thing: *WE GAVE THE CASH REWARD IN FIVE $2 BILLS.*

103

BLOCKBUSTER
How To Build A Million Dollar Tax Business

We'd go to the bank at the end of each week during tax season and get a big stack of two-dollar bills. And each Saturday, we'd mail a thank you letter with the cash inside for all the people who referred their friends from the previous week. Of course, the first thing you are thinking to yourself, "Why are you sending cash in the mail? Nobody does that." EXACTLY! That's one of the main reasons our referral program would spread to so many other people. We did stuff no other tax businesses in our area would do and the word-of-mouth would expand accordingly.

But the **TWO-DOLLAR BILL STRATEGY made the word-of-mouth about our tax business spread even more!** When people open an envelope and pull out a handful of $2 bills, it's so unusual that getting this money in the mail becomes an experience. And once you WOW someone, they will talk about you and your business even more.

And as part of the referral "training" for our clients, we'd say IN THE THANK YOU LETTER, "When you go to spend these $2 bills and people ask you where you got them, please smile and say MY tax pro sent them to me in the mail!"

This just adds more fuel to the word-of-mouth fire.

So the faster you can reward your referring clients (in the middle of tax season) with CASH – especially with $2 bills -- the more your tax business will come up as an option to help folks file their taxes.

Don't send a check.

It's cash or something different. Do not do a discount off your services, either. This gesture does NOT help at all. Clients don't see it as a reward, and a discount does not help spread the word-of-mouth effectively.

BLOCKBUSTER
How To Build A Million Dollar Tax Business

If not cash, try something different – dinner for two, or tickets to a movie. There are plenty of creative options. We would work out deals with area retailers. I bought gifts in bulk which had a $20 or $30 value, but only cost us $5 or $10. So you choose whatever you want to do. The point is having a good incentive to encourage referrals.

At the end of the day, if your client feels like they were appreciated for their referral actions, they will do it again. (And that's the main point.)

Now, what if you don't want to compensate them? What if you can't send them money or you don't want to send a financial reward?

A very powerful word-of-mouth stimulator which generates plenty of referrals is a handwritten note. You taking the time to write a handwritten note to somebody thanking them for their business during tax season is huge. A lot of times this personal gesture can be more powerful than any money. A $50 bill is nice. But a personal handwritten note will bring back more quality referred clients.

NOTE: How to make sending handwritten notes a practical word-of-mouth strategy: Actually get them done when you are in your busy season. Want to be able to personally write hundreds or even thousands of hand-written notes, get them signed and delivered in the mail quickly? I've used **Send Out Cards** in the past. I recommend this company because once you set everything up (send them your handwriting samples) the whole process is turn-key. I won't go into the details here. Just Google them and give them a try.

For your small-business clients worth several thousand dollars to you annually, get a part-time employee in your office to be the point person for delivering gifts. Here's something that's really cool and works like gangbusters for women: deliver a little bouquet of flowers to her workplace the day after she came to your office. Make sure that the delivery company shows up in the middle of the day, right up front, where everybody in the office sees it. "Oh, who gave you flowers?" "Oh, these are from my accountant." "Why did he do that?" "Well, I just referred _____." (You get the point.) THE SAME STRATEGY WORKS FOR GUYS. Just deliver something other than flowers.

Something else that works way better than people give it credit for: candy. Just a simple, corny gesture where you write a little note. "You are so sweet to refer some of your friends our way, we thought you'd like some chocolate." Then stick the candy with the note in the mail. The envelope will have a bulge in it from the chocolate, which means your letter will get opened faster and remembered longer. I've seen folks mail a small M&M packet of candy that costs hardly anything – but gets great results! People remember you and they refer others to you. That's the point. You're doing simple follow-up techniques that nobody else in the tax industry does. I promise your competition will not do this.

Even The Best Referral Program Won't Work When ...

Over the years, I've heard stories from a couple of my tax business owner clients who used some of these referral strategies and they didn't work. Turns out, these tax pros were not personable. They gave horrific service. They were unorganized. They did a bad job of actually preparing the tax return. Then they couldn't understand why nobody was referring new clients to them.

Sounds obvious. But let me be clear. I'm assuming you offer a good tax service ... that you're very good at what you do ... that you take care of your clients ... and that because of your desire to be a high quality tax professional, others will naturally want to refer you.

When you do the basics in your tax service business, you are going to get some referrals. But everything else I've talked about will help inject a whole new level of word-of-mouth spreading in your community about your tax practice.

Once you begin to proactively promote a Referral Culture among your clients, the first years (especially years two and three) you'll see a very nice bump in business. At the four- and five-year mark, your clients will get it. A *Culture* will have been established and YOUR EXISTING CLIENTS will DO much of the "training" of the new clients for you. This is when your RAF program is on money-making auto-pilot.

A System for Referral Marketing

Actually, having the System in place to help implement the marketing is critically important. So before you ever have a chance to promote your Refer-A-Friend Program, you have what I call a front-end marketing funnel. These are all of the advertising campaigns targeted to various groups of people most likely to want to do business with your tax practice. (Hint: Did you know some types of people are more inclined to give your referrals compared to other groups?) We'll come back to this in a minute.

One front-end marketing funnel could be TV. Another broadcast media marketing funnel is radio. A big part of your front-end marketing should be direct mail.

BLOCKBUSTER
How To Build A Million Dollar Tax Business

A mailing to a certain target demographic living in a three-mile radius around your tax office would be a simple but effective example. Even treating your existing clients as a target group and mailing their neighbors is a doable strategy.

HOW YOU BRING NEW PROSPECTS INTO YOUR FRONT END MARKETING FUNNEL MATTERS.

Now, for the sake of this conversation, let's focus on tax season. But everything I'm sharing applies to year-round marketing as well.

In order to systemize your marketing, you must start with a *Promotional Calendar*.

But before you begin picking dates for your advertising campaigns, from a strategy point of view, what kind of person is most likely to refer you to others if you do a great job preparing their taxes?

This is an important question to answer. If you fill your practice with new clients this tax season who are three times more likely to refer their friends, versus a regular tax client, which new client is more valuable to you? Of course, the hyper-referral client.

The best way to identify your current hyper-referring clients is to look in your database and handpick a couple dozen clients who refer plenty of business on an annual basis.

Chances are good you'll notice commonalities: their occupation, hobbies, charities they give to and even their personal ambitions (if you know them well enough).

Getting back to my question I just asked a little earlier ...

From my experience and from the success stories my coaching clients tell me about, some of **the BEST word-of-mouth groups to work with are connected to your local Rescue Squad, Fire Fighters and Police Officers.**

These public servants (including the volunteers) work so hard helping our communities. When they find a tax professional who goes the extra mile and takes care of them, these folks and their families are so grateful. And believe me; they KNOW how to get the word out in the community. If you (as a tax pro) "have their back" with Uncle Sam, these hard working men and women will continuously feed your tax practice new referrals for years and years.

Tax Business Marketing Calendar

Now that you know who you want to target, planning a marketing calendar will ensure you execute your promotional strategy to help you maximize your resources and steward your time.

I recommend printing out the first four months of the year and placing four sheets of paper on your desk. There's about 100 days on the four pages where you'll focus your energy.

Start by attaching the times when you will communicate with your existing clients. (This is the most important target list because they are the core referral stimulators.) Next is your "lost" list. These are past clients who, for whatever reason, never came back to you. Go back three years and compile this list. I usually add my Lost Client promos on my marketing calendar the week after I mail or email my existing clients. (Don't just send your clients one mailing at the beginning of tax season. You'll surely leave many referrals "on the table" if that's all you do!)

The next set of campaigns you'll add to your marketing calendar will be those target niches you've identified as more likely to refer other quality clients. Then, group-by-group, keep going down your list and insert actual time and dates into your marketing calendar.

If you are serious about implementing multiple marketing promotions during tax season, you must schedule everything in advance. If you don't, you know what will happen. Tax season comes along and your marketing plan gets "punted" because you were too busy.

Once you've blocked time in your schedule, it's just as if you're meeting with a tax client. You are not going to miss this appointment. So during your marketing appointments, you show up and get those ads done! (I highly recommend hiring a part-time marketing assistant to execute everything you have set up on the dates you've scheduled these promotions.)

Once you have your marketing referral stimulator calendar scheduled, remember to use multiple forms of media. So, instead of mailing your clients three letters about referring their friends, I'd mail one letter, and in three days email a similar message; then, a week later, follow up with a post card – all mentioning each step, but promoting the same message a little differently.

Have some fun with the delivery of your marketing messages. HOW you ask for referrals can give your word-of-mouth business a real boost as well. Include funny pictures that help tell a compelling story. Add eye-catching color. Since I'm color blind, I use NEON colors on post cards all the time. They always worked better than a regular white post card. Size matters, too. We'd design an 11 x 17 post card and call it "The World's Biggest Tax Business Referral Coupon." People loved these and passed them around to their friends like hot cakes!

Obviously, social media also can be very helpful in spreading the word about your tax business. However, it has been my experience that MOST tax pros (when using Facebook or Twitter as an example) miss the opportunity for creativity. No one really pays attention to them.

Have some fun with it. I encourage my tax business owner clients to use these various social media platforms to showcase their most excited clients. This is easier than ever nowadays.

<u>Require every employee in your office to pull out their smart phone and record a client on-the-spot when they say something nice about you or show enthusiasm towards your tax service business.</u>

Even better, have a contest of "WHO CAN GIVE THE BEST VIDEO TESTIMONIAL" while they are in your office. (If they leave without recording a video, you'll miss your chance.)

When your tax business' online presence is LOADED with people on video saying how great you are, the preponderance of proof is overwhelming. Taxpayers who have never heard of you will believe the sheer volume of real people on these video testimonials and come do business with you. This is just another form of stimulating referrals.

The Featured Third Party Endorsement

You can take this referral thing to the next level and feature a few of your best-referring clients in an actual advertisement. I call these folks champion clients. (Every tax practice has them.)

Years ago, our record was the client who referred 71 new people in one tax season! The guy literally would bring new clients to our office door, walk them in and make sure we knew he referred them to our tax business. (Now that's a champion!)

Feature one or more champion clients (your top three is best) in a series of ads. Highlight their stories in your weekly emails. Add their picture and a curiosity headline on a postcard. Insert them on a flier in one of your sales letters. Shoot a "man-on-the-street" style video and post it on your main website.

My point is you have these incredible assets in your tax business. Pull them INTO THE OPEN and USE these champions to bring head-turning attention to your tax business.

Strategic Alliance Referral Team

Another high-level referral process involves being even more purposeful and strategic. This kind of strategy takes extra time and effort, but it's well worth it. These types of referrals are worth three, four, five, ... up to ten times more than the other referrals because they're professionals referring professionals. This strategy is setting up your own Strategic Alliance Referral Team.

As you know, the most profitable new clients come from other professionals who recommend their clients to you. So anybody in a related business in your city (you probably already have connections with some of them) could be on your "team." I'm talking about insurance agents, mortgage brokers, financial planners and any other kinds of investment professionals. There are so many different professionals who complement the tax industry; just start making a list.

Most tax professionals fail to cultivate relationships with other related pros because it takes extra time to be intentional about working with each other. They want to work with you. You want to work with them. So it's time for you to take the bull by the horns and go out there and have a conversation with a few of these financial professionals.

Once you go through the initial legwork of compiling a list of professional services and contact info, it's all downhill from there. It's a little front-end loaded, but once you send over a few referrals and start receiving a couple in return, you'll see these relationships become valuable wells of ongoing revenue for many years to come.

Key Point: You've got to have a compelling reason for these service professionals to choose you to work with versus some other tax pro down the street. What's your Unique Selling Proposition? Why should THIS TYPE OF PRO refer his/her clients to you versus every other option available to them?

Now I'm not going to get into the financial compensation issue here. There are laws or rules about what you can and can't do in your state and with your professional license. But I will tell you there's some serious passive income to be made here if you're permitted to do so.

Next Steps

I would encourage you to set up a process to build a formal team of strategic alliances. You will scratch their backs, and they will reciprocate. All you do is put together a simple inquiry letter. You mail it on day one. Follow up with an email on day three. Then make a quick phone call on day five asking, "Did you get my letter and email this week?"

Do this with fifteen or twenty professionals. It's not a big list. The follow-up when you get them on the phone is ten minutes. Set up a lunch meeting or even have them come to your office for an exploratory meeting. If it makes sense and you both want to work together, then great; set up a separate meeting a week later to brainstorm the best ways to help each other.

By the way, it doesn't hurt for you to bring references and testimonials about you. This will shorten the time it takes to build trust with one another. (They will provide references back to you once you've taken this initial step.)

There's low hanging fruit in EVERY database. So pretty quickly you each can get started making money from each other's list. After you get over that first referral hump, you're off to the races.

I recommend you build a dream team. Set up a win-win-win. Try to carve out a circle of maybe five professionals covering a variety of different financial services in your area. Then you'll enjoy a steady stream of referrals. When you align with the right professionals, this is a truly powerful strategy.

The Maven Strategy

<u>Mavens are an untapped referral source for most tax business owners</u>. My definition of a Maven: He or she is an expert, somebody who is a **leader in his or her field with a strong influence over others.** Everyone knows people like this. Think about the "connecting" people in your town, in your city, in your community, in your marketplace, wherever you do business. Think about the men and women other people clearly look to. They have influence.

Most of these Mavens are NOT going to be your existing tax clients. However, that doesn't need to stop you; Mavens like helping people find answers to their problems. If you work out an arrangement with them, they will endorse you to everyone they know. (And these folks know a lot of people!)

Truth be told, the Mavens with real influence don't even want to be compensated by you. They don't want to do any special deals. But I still recommend you do something for these Mavens who prefer not to be compensated. Mail them some free tickets to "the game" or dinner and a movie each month as a nice gesture to show your appreciation. (Well worth the small investment!)

Compile a list of probably twenty-five potential Mavens in your area. I'd work this small group of names with a simple follow-up monthly marketing funnel. The key is to remind them you are out there helping people with their taxes. (Mavens will connect the dots.)

Oh, and the 80/20 Rule is alive here as well. If you're working with ten Mavens, two are going to be superstars for you, and the other eight will be "okay." If you need more Mavens to actually send you prospects, expect results based on the 80/20 formula. So if your plan requires at least ten influential leaders referring new clients your way, you'll need to formalize that plan with fifty to start. It's just a math game at this point.

So in conclusion, I'll just say this:

The number one marketing focus you always start with is your existing clients. They are the acres of diamonds in your backyard. Those are the ones you pour into first. Now, do you do other marketing campaigns? Absolutely. But you start with the people already paying you money and have some level of relationship with you.

Get a vision for a year-round approach. Talk about them in your newsletter. Feature some of your clients because they referred a lot of new clients to you. People will say, "How do I get in the newsletter? I want to be featured." Your answer is simple: "You've got to refer more people."

BLOCKBUSTER
How To Build A Million Dollar Tax Business

Everything discussed here connects to building a Referral Culture in your tax business.

Most of all, have some fun with it and you WILL see a significant boost in your new clients' sales.

Chapter 8

Tax Biz Wealth Is In
THE PROCESS

Wealth is ultimately built and sustained from the processes you operate in your tax business.

Every tax business owner has at least one core competency. And those same tax practices have a process for providing whatever services are offered in the business. Some processes might be weak, vulnerable and caustic to the practice, but others could be the golden ticket for adding profit to the bottom line every week. Yes, all processes are not created equal.

Is your tax business an event-driven business or is it a process-driven business?

An event-driven business deals with whatever comes up as it happens. You randomly work on your client's tax information based on when they need it and the urgency of other projects in your office. You take care of your clients as best as you can. There's always something waiting for you to do.

<u>A process-driven business follows a series of exact steps done in the same order and the same way every time.</u>

BLOCKBUSTER
How To Build A Million Dollar Tax Business

There's no randomness. No spontaneity. Everyone in the office follows these steps or there are negative consequences. The processes in this kind of tax practice are easily replicated.

But in the tax industry, most tax business owners make themselves the center of the process by default. Everything runs through them: tax questions, phone inquiries, computer problems, software glitches. (I could go on, but you get the idea.)

When issues good or bad arise, everyone in the office has to run it through the owner. This creates an unnecessary ceiling that keeps MANY tax practices from growing and making any significant money.

And here's the reality check:

Big money breakthroughs cannot take place in this environment.

If you, as the owner, are the problem because most of your office runs through you and you don't have a series of exact steps which are done in the same order in a systematic fashion in your office, THEN **THIS IS A RED FLAG**.

Now, I'm not talking about every little detail. But I am talking about the most important areas of your tax office. Sooner or later, you'll have to deal with this; it may as well be now.

Let me give you some examples that may happen in your office:

Getting a new client to call your office and set up an appointment. Helping someone when they walk into your lobby area. Making sure additional fees are properly charged for your services. Providing high quality tax preparation in an efficient manner. Hiring an experienced employee. Running an effective advertising campaign.

THESE ARE ALL <u>EVENTS</u> IN
YOUR BUSINESS.

The huge wealth creation question is,

"Do you have a <u>PROCESS</u> to go with these events?"

If you desire these events to run smoothly and bring good results, you must build a standing process for EACH. In other words, a process is a System.

A System is an overused word in the tax industry. Tax business owners SAY they have systems in their offices. But in truth, few tax pros follow a systematic process in their office.

How to Build A Process

Get a separate sheet of paper. I'm going to give you a few examples. Then I'd like you to write down the How, When, Where, Why, What, Who and By Whom for each of these examples.

This is how you begin building a foundation of processes in your tax business.

On your sheet of paper, I'd like you to answer each of these seven questions (How? When? Where? Why? What? Who? By Whom?) PER EVENT. (I gave you some event examples earlier in this chapter.)

One of those Event Examples was:

- Helping someone when they enter your lobby area.

How does that work in your office? What will someone do? When will this person be helped and by Whom? Who else might jump in and provide service? Why? What happens next? And so on.

Do you get what's happening here? By answering these questions, it's forcing you to review all of the possible angles of a particular event that happens all the time in your office. Each key event is important for the overall success of your tax practice.

To truly systemize your tax office with a step-by-step process, you must break down EACH important event into bite-sized steps, and each person in your office will follow them until they become second nature.

Once you decide on the "right-way" for your office, you'll need to set up tracking procedures to measure what success looks like. The first year you'll probably figure out the benchmarks. After that, setting goals will be your next step for improving your overall efficient and effective office flow.

Your Main Goal

As the owner of your tax business, your main goal is to get someone else to handle each event in your office BETTER than you would ever be able to do. Once your employees are delivering excellent service by following each of the main processes you've put into place, the office can run at peak efficiency, even when you're NOT in the building.

Many tax business owners don't believe this scenario could ever be possible for them. You say you're sick and tired of doing all the work. But when push comes to shove, too many times the owner is unwilling to take the not-so-hard-next-steps that free them from the chains of their tax business's operational jail.

I can speak from personal experience. It was better for everyone in our tax offices for me to get out of the way and let my staff do their thing. I hired them to use their particular talents and skills. These employees are good; they wouldn't be there otherwise. And this way there are less headaches and stress for me. Isn't this what's supposed to happen when you truly systemize your tax office?

Yes, it is.

So if you are still being a bottleneck for your tax office's operational flow, it's time to take a look in the mirror and make the decision once and for all to allow your tax business to grow without you holding on to every little detail so tightly.

Once you let go, and invest in other people working for you (following the processes you have set up for them), your tax business will begin to shift to the next level of success. The more you hold on, the longer the next level of success will escape you.

Remember, look at ALL of the most important events in your office. How best to charge higher fees per return. How to provide a better quality tax preparation experience. How to recruit and hire more experienced tax preparers. How to compile and write the most effective advertising campaigns.

I recommend you write down at least ten other events you believe are key to your tax business' success and start building processes for them.

BLOCKBUSTER
How To Build A Million Dollar Tax Business

You Are <u>Not</u> In The TAX Business

The core competency for most tax pros is preparing tax returns. That's okay. You got into this business because you're good at solving tax problems for people. But if you want to attract higher levels of revenue, know that wealth flows into your tax business from OTHER activities – not from doing the actual work of accounting or tax preparation.

If you didn't realize it already, let me break the news to you. You are NOT in the tax business. <u>If you want to take your tax practice to a much higher, profitable level</u>, get it in your head that **YOU ARE IN THE "MARKETING AND ADVERTISING OF YOUR TAX PRACTICE" BUSINESS.**

I hope you can see that!

Generating Qualified Prospects To Contact Your Office So You Can Sell Your Tax Services To Them ... As The Owner, THIS MUST BE YOUR CORE JOB.

Your core competency must now shift to include overseeing the most important money-making activities in your business: Marketing ... Advertising ... Selling ... Recruiting and Hiring Quality Staff ... Pricing and Structuring Fees.

This includes assuming the sale and converting these interested people or prospects into someone who actually comes into your office and uses your tax services. Once sitting with your preparer, they agree to all the additional services recommend for their situation.

Now, your margins are high, and every new client is happy with what they're getting from your staff. Then because they feel good, these new clients take the next step and tell other people about you and your tax services. Leading this kind of operation is the BEST core competency to have for a successful tax practice.

As the owner, focusing your attention on setting up strategic alliances, third-party endorsements, and other joint venture opportunities in your community is a valuable use of your time. (The difference between this kind of activity and sitting behind a desk and preparing a tax return is like night and day.)

You are the "flag-waver" of your business. Improving your Referral Program goes a long way to finding new clients you might never have reached unless your client passed them one of your referral fliers. They're "spreading the gospel" about you and your ability to handle complex tax returns and keep the IRS off your back. These kinds of powerful new client attraction promotions don't just happen randomly.

To maximize their effectiveness, your leadership as the owner is critical.

The Missing Link is in the PROCESS

Here's the important wealth attraction insight I want you to get. Your marketing, salesmanship, recruiting, hiring, training, pricing strategies, and most every other important area are NOT performing to the level you know they could BECAUSE YOU ARE MISSING THE PROCESS.

If you put the right processes in place in all of these areas, your tax practice will go from an Event-Driven Business to a PROCESS-Driven, Well-Oiled Machine. When everyone in your business follows established, successful processes every time –

your tax business will produce more wealth automatically. And not just in one location. Once one tax office's profit flows like a river, you will seriously consider opening more locations.

Your Decision Making

Another way you can attract wealth and improve your office processes is through better, faster, more efficient daily decision-making. During a fast-paced tax season, being decisive in your actions is absolutely necessary. Once you get personal clarity on how you want to prioritize your decisions, then you can be decisive.

Here's a second exercise: I'd like you to consider seven questions. All of these relate to how you make decisions. Make notes for yourself as to which way you lean on each.

#1

When an opportunity presents itself, do you ask yourself a) Will this make the best use of my talents and strengths? or b) Will this need me to do things that I'm not really good at, requiring a significant learning curve?

#2

Does the opportunity a) fit my personal preferences, or b) not fit with my personal preferences?

#3

Does the opportunity a) leverage my existing assets and resources, or b) require n*ew resources to do it?*

So for example, if you're in tax season and an opportunity arises and you have existing assets and resources in place to make it happen, but you'd have to go out and acquire some new skills pretty fast, maybe it's not the best time to say yes.

Let's push pause for a second.

What I'm doing here is giving you a short-cut check list on how best to make decisions. WE ARE TURNING THE BIGGER CHOICES YOU MAKE INTO A PROCESS. Again, anything that's important to your tax business must have a process in place to help you become more successful.

If you don't do some version of what I'm describing, then you'll just waste time or be less decisive, or make poor decisions. Bad choices can cost more than you realize. Just the opportunity costs of some decisions can set you back one or two tax seasons while your competition charges ahead of you.

#4

Does this opportunity have a) a minimum level of acceptance, or b) some uncertainty or difficulty to implement?

#5

If I say yes to this decision, a) is delegation possible, or b) do I have to do all the work?

Side Note: This is a biggie for me. As the owner, I delegate almost everything. So if I have to do too much of the work to get something done, my answer will usually be no.

#6

Will this decision a) produce a repeatable process and enhance the overall business value, or b) be a one-time gain, nice payday, and then be done?

#7

Will doing this a) give me or my business positive associations, or b) involve negative associations?

So, at the end of the day, is a particular opportunity going to help me based on who we're associated with professionally and personally, or is it going impact me and my tax business in a negative way down the road?

Once you compile a Check List similar to these questions, you will have made a new decision-making process for your tax practice.

<u>You will be more decisive and make better decisions as a result.</u>

Could You NOT SHOW UP During Tax Season For Three Weeks?

Again, tax professionals talk a really good game about systems and how important they are in their business. But when I've done on-site consultations for my coaching clients, what is said over the phone versus the reality of their office can be worlds apart.

Your goal should be to make your tax office run more smoothly WITHOUT you being involved in the daily operations in any way. So if you decided to leave town for several weeks during tax season, your tax business wouldn't miss a beat. Note: When you decide to sell your business, you will get a much higher number when your tax office is NOT owner operated.

What if you were FORCED to not be in your office during tax season? What if health issues arise at the busiest time of your year? What then? Over the years, I can count on two hands the number of my clients who have had to go into the hospital in the middle of tax season because of health problems. A health emergency is never on someone's to-do list.

I've also heard stories of tax business owners losing their practice because they "got sick" and couldn't work during tax season. Since the majority of the workload ran through them, most everything was left hanging and the clients went elsewhere. Other times, the tax pro couldn't work for three to six weeks. The owner fell so far behind that the business's overall profit suffered greatly as a result.

Consider another, very instructive (and encouraging) side to stories like this.

The same type of "illness" scenario happened. But in a few cases, true silver linings came forth and changed several tax business owners' lives for the better. I'm paraphrasing several of my tax-business-owner clients' stories together to make a point.

In the middle of tax season, the owner could not be in the office for weeks or months. Little-to-no contact was made back to the staff. The employees had to "figure it out" the best they could. And guess what happened? The sky didn't fall!

To the surprise of each tax business owner, their employees did the best they could and the tax practice continued on making money, bringing in new clients and serving previous clients. The owner didn't have to be involved in "everything" like they thought they did. And a beautiful thing happened. When these owners came back slowly to work in their offices, they continued to let their staff run the business for them. And as it turns out, this is what the owners always wanted, but were unwilling to let go and delegate most of the workload.

(Which is probably why they had the illness during tax season.)

The moral of the story is:

Don't be FORCED to delegate the majority of your workload. Set up your processes now so your employees can run your business the way you want it run.

(That way you can leave your office when you want, driving yourself, instead of having someone else give you a ride in an emergency vehicle.)

Automate Your Tax Business

Lastly, I want to talk about how best to automate as much of your tax office operations as you can. If you will allow automation to systemize your practice for you, the key processes you most want to happen in your daily operations will have a much greater chance of being implemented.

I break tax office operations down into three sections: Front, Middle and Back. I do this to simplify the roles of each position in our office.

When clients walk into the front section of a tax office, everyone is clear on what's supposed to be done. In the middle of the office, where the tax preparation is handled, the same thing applies. And then we want to make sure all of our services are being executed properly. So in the back we're checking over the returns, processing the work and implementing all of the follow-up procedures.

But what if you could automate as much of this as possible?

Well, you can.

Another successful tax business owner has already done it for you. It's called The Automated Tax Office Manager (ATOM). I highly recommend ATOM software for your tax practice.

If you're interested in learning more, go here.

www.MillionDollarTaxBiz.com/ATOM

The big take-away is this:

You already have some processes in your office that you're going to use. But when you step up to a higher level of automation in your office, you as the owner can delegate or oversee SO much more because of this technology.

Not only will you become a better manager of your office, but you'll do everything much faster and more efficiently – which equals more money in your pocket!

Chapter 9

Effective Tax Biz Leadership Dramatically Reduces Your Stress And Headaches

The tax industry is void of quality leadership.

Tax business owners are notorious for running their practices by either "doing it themselves" or spending very little time mentoring and training staff to successfully handle the operational flow of their office.

Your tax practice can make some significant strides and have a real impact on your community, city, or even region if you improve your leadership.

By the same token, when poor leadership is in place, unnecessary stress and headaches appear. The tax industry has "accepted" the fact that during the busiest season of the year, you are supposed to be stressed out.

In my view, you don't have to accept headaches as a way of life during tax season.

Let me tell you a quick story about one of the best leaders I've ever met. He taught me so much of "what to do" and "how to be" a great leader in life.

BLOCKBUSTER
How To Build A Million Dollar Tax Business

Back in the late 1990's our tax business was approaching the two-million-dollars-per-tax-season sales mark. When attending a particular success seminar I met the "consultant's consultant." His name was Somers White. He was a high-level guy helping professionals from all over the world to get better at whatever they needed in business.

However, Somers's specialty was in management and leadership. He was THE Guru.

I hired him to spend a couple of days with me to work on improving our tax business. But you're probably asking, "Chauncey, you were already doing a couple million dollars in sales ... What needed improvement?" Well as it turns out, a lot!

Remember, I wasn't hiring Somers for marketing or sales issues. This wasn't our problem. I needed help with the operations. I'd never run a multi-location organization before, so I was definitely looking for management help and everything that comes along with it.

I spent almost a month preparing for my meeting with this management and leadership guru. I prepared about 30 pages of notes for our two day meeting. Since I was flying all the way across the country and paying a "pretty penny" for this guru's time, I wanted to be a good steward of this opportunity.

Now the first day of our meeting was finally here. In the first hour, Somers began by asking me a series of questions about our tax business. I gave my best answers, but I could see I was in trouble. Then in the second hour, we covered even more ground about our operations and what we did in different situations as we grew.

After the second hour with Somers White, we took a little break. I looked down at my 30 pages of notes and ripped them up and threw them in the trash. I knew right then and there I needed to start over. My view of leading our family business was completely off. I was asking all the wrong questions. I was missing SO many details. I realized in that moment that our tax business needed a complete overhaul. And the revamp needed to start at the top, right behind my two eyeballs!

Somers taught me a whole new way to lead and manage an organization. Once I was able to get my mind around what he was telling me (it took a little while to get my thinking straight), I bought into what he was saying and agreed with him on a plan to move forward.

If No One Is Following You ... You're Not Leading

The best way to lead and manage your tax practice is through clear, simple and easy-to-follow steps. Employees must be able to understand what you are trying to accomplish. How you communicate with them is paramount.

So if you're trying to lead your staff and they are not following you very well, then chances are good you're not being the best leader you can be.

Simplicity is one of the keys to leadership success. I was slow to learn this lesson. I wanted to over- complicate things and move my agenda at a super-fast pace. Now there's nothing wrong with executing your tax business's strategic plan as quickly as possible. Again, issues arise when the execution is not broken down into simple, doable steps for others to accomplish.

Leaders have a clear vision where the organization is going (your tax business) and they are equipped to oversee and supervise the people who are making this vision happen.

Supervision sees what's going well and what's not going so well. As the supervisor, if the wrong processes and procedures are happening in your tax office, it's your job to straighten it out. It's called Accountability.

Accountability seems to be a taboo word in many tax professional circles. But if you don't have rewards and consequences (which is what accountability really is) you can't be an effective leader. <u>Holding the people who work for you accountable is the only way to systematically improve your office over the long haul.</u>

Which brings us to management. **A manager is someone who knows how to get things done through other people.** When you're wearing your manager hat, you'll get your hands dirty in more of the details. But you'll also know what's missing in your process and what needs to change in order to move forward. Many times in your managerial role you'll see a quality employee struggling. Chances are you have them in the wrong role. Use wisdom as a leader to match their gifts and talents with a job description your tax business needs the most.

Many times, being a good leader comes down to finding the right job that fits each employee. Once your staff is working in the best roles for them, providing clear expectations with agreed-upon follow-up benchmarks (for accountability) makes for an excellent office environment for everyone: The owner, the employees, and the clients being served.

The Four Powers of Leadership

Effective leadership boils down to these four things: The Power in *Simplicity*. The Power in *Clarity*. The Power in *Asking Questions* (and actually listening to the answers). And, The Power of *Time*.

As the owner, if you want to increase your employee buy-in, his or her motivation, his or her attitude, AND if you want to improve how your tax business executes – then WHAT you say and HOW you say it is important.

This is Strategy.

You can move forward in your tax business in many different ways. And truthfully, there are plenty of right answers because much of what you are deciding is based on your (the owner's) personal preference because it's your business.

Here's my favorite real world example and probably my most effective way of implementing The Four Powers of Leadership:

You read a book on How to Build a Million Dollar Tax Business. You get a ton of new ideas and insights on how to run a more successful tax practice. But how do you go from your "pages of notes" to implementing these new strategies within your tax office?

Use the **"Three Best, Three Worst, Three Changes" Leadership Technique.**

Here's how to go from Point A (where you are now) to Point B (where you want to end up):

BLOCKBUSTER
How To Build A Million Dollar Tax Business

Call a meeting for a week from today. Ask your employees (let's say there are five people working for you) to block off one hour in their schedule for next Thursday morning at 10:00 a.m.

You tell them you want to grow, improve and run a more successful tax practice. That's what the meeting is all about. But before you meet, tell them you want their feedback. Plus, tell your staff you want their answers sent back to you in a certain format and at a certain time.

Tell them to email you 24 hours before the meeting begins (by Wednesday 10:00 a.m.). Then, ask them to give you their perspective on the following:

What are the three BEST things happening in our tax practice?

What are the three WORST things happening from your perspective?

What three CHANGES* would you like to see made to improve this business?

*Each change must include a plan for HOW you would implement these changes.

Remind your employees, that you are only looking for THREE of each category. Write as much as you need to on each item, but send feedback on the top three only. Also say, if you submit one of your changes without an explanation on how you'd recommend making the change, then the change will NOT be considered.

Then on Tuesday, send another email reminding your employees of the 10:00 a.m. deadline on Wednesday. (If someone does not submit their feedback by the deadline, there should be consequences.) If they are not going to take seriously this very important meeting you've scheduled, then maybe they should work someplace else.

I'm going to assume for this example that all five employees emailed you their feedback on time. For a leader, one day in advance is important. (I'll explain why in a minute.)

Now from everyone on your team, you have their Three Best, Three Worst & Three Changes, PLUS, How each person would implement the changes they listed.

That means you have compiled into one document, a full day before your meeting begins, 15 Good Things about your tax business, 15 Not-So-Good Things, and 15 Recommended Changes from the people who work in your business on what they believe would make your tax business more successful. And better yet, you'll have about seven or eight decent ideas on how you can implement the best way to make these changes happen moving forward.

Okay, armed with this info one full day BEFORE your employee meeting begins, do you think you have some power as a leader? The answer is yes. You have a tremendous amount of power because you know ahead of time what every single employee is thinking (good, bad and ugly) and how they would go about making important changes in your business.

THIS IS HUGE!

As a leader, it's an incredible way to clarify the skills and talents of each person working for you. You also get a feel for your employees' attitudes and detect whether any "issues" are bubbling up under the surface in your office. This is very helpful because you can stomp out the smoldering problems before they turn into out-of-control fires wrecking your office's operations.

And just for the record: 80 percent of everything your employees write down will not be new info for you. That's okay. It's the other 20 percent that you'll need to pay more attention to.

Oh, and don't spend a ton of time on the "bad stuff" happening in your office. The main reason for discussing all of this info in the meeting is NOT to allow a whining session to take place. You ask for a Worst List from your employees to help them buy into the reality that they will be the ones implementing the changes to correct these wrong things in your business.

NOTE: Before I get too far, let me give you a heads-up about frequency. <u>This will not be the only time you use this Three Best, Three Worst, Three Changes Structure for meetings in your business</u>. I'd recommend having a meeting similar to this on a monthly basis.

Over time, you will cut off many problems before they become big and it'll save you a ton of headaches, stress and hassle.

Once you've reviewed the Best, Worst and Changes, most of your time will be spent on discussing HOW these changes can get implemented. Cap this meeting at one hour, but before you finish, schedule the next meeting for a week later.

That whole meeting will be on HOW TO EXECUTE THE CHANGES THAT EVERYONE IN THE OFFICE AGREED UPON NEEDS TO HAPPEN IN YOUR TAX BUSINESS.

This is a big deal because when everyone "buys in" and takes part in the solution, a tremendous shift takes place in your office environment. You lead better and your staff has someone to follow!

Eighty Percent of the Meeting Happens BEFORE The Meeting

As you can see, the majority of the work is completed before the meeting even begins. The same is true for the follow up to the first meeting.

Again, you will ask your employees to write down Three Specific Steps they see as most important for accomplishing EACH of the Top Three Changes. You'll also ask your staff to compile the Three Road Blocks (issues that might come up when trying to make these changes) most likely to happen amongst the team. And finally, have them provide their recommendations on HOW to overcome these Road Blocks to ensure success.

Do you see a pattern here?

Now we're getting into the nitty-gritty, which (in the real world) is where success happens! As the leader of this next meeting, you'll have full access to everyone's ideas, plans and how best to achieve the goals you set up. Again, it is extremely valuable to have this info before going into the follow up meeting a week later.

At the completion of the second meeting, not only will you have <u>Agreement On Three Main Changes You Want To See Happen in Your Tax Business, But Also A Specific Action List For Each Of The Three Main Goals</u>. **Set A Goal for Each Change So Everyone Is Clear on What Success Looks Like In the End**. These action points have deadlines for completion and someone (not you) from your office that is responsible for completing each task.

Note: This will be easier than you think because most times you're assigning the task to the person who raised the issue in the first place and offered the best solution for fixing the problem.

Your role as the leader (owner) of the tax business is to hold everyone else accountable for doing what they have agreed on doing.

This is leadership. It's your money. It's your business. It's your name. This is how you oversee the growth process, but with you not having to do everything. As the owner, you need time to think. You must clear time in your schedule to make good, wise decisions and allow yourself the proper amount of time to follow up with your employees. With over 80 percent of the workload on the shoulders of your staff, this will allow you more time to be a better leader through supervision and management.

Extra Advice About Running Your Meetings

I recommend you compile all of your employees' feedback into one document removing their names from their input. You'll want everyone in your office to see what the team as a whole is saying about the business. But you only want to do so about five minutes before the meeting begins. (It will help make sure everyone shows up a few minutes early.)

This meeting document needs to be organized by category. All the good stuff, all the bad stuff and all the changes – plus the follow up section on how these changes are to be implemented.

BLOCKBUSTER
How To Build A Million Dollar Tax Business

Assign each section a certain number of minutes to discuss as a group. Let's say you start with 10 minutes to review all the Best Things happening inside your business. I'd assign 15 minutes for the Worst Things. When leading this section, don't get into the "What Needs To Change" --those conversations are coming next. Just get clarification on what your employees mean when bringing up their not-so-good list. Lastly, discuss the TOP CHANGES NEEDING TO BE MADE, and let employees speak freely on HOW they'd make these changes happen in the context of your business. I recommend 25 minutes for this section.

Stick to this schedule. Don't let certain employees dominate the discussion. Make sure everyone gets a turn to speak up and offer feedback. Once you add a five- minute introduction (give vision for why you're having this meeting) and a five-minute conclusion (our next steps will be a follow-up meeting at this particular time) and thank and encourage everyone for taking this process of improving our tax business seriously, then you end your meeting ON TIME at the 60-minute mark.

Remember: Before the end of the day, you can email your staff the specific follow-up info you want them to compile for the next meeting. Remind them of the date and time you want this information. Then you repeat this structure all over again.

You're going to see your best employees rise to the surface through this process. So if there are five people working for you, as the 80/20 rule states, one of them is going to be the sharpest and have the best answers. That one will be assigned the most important projects. But there will also be somebody else in your office that totally doesn't get it. They are unengaged and you can see it in their answers. Their follow-up is weak and the energy they bring to the table is low.

By leading your staff in such a practical way, they're going to weed themselves out (if you don't end up doing it first) because this is not what they signed up for. They don't want to be a part of a business that's trying to be more successful. They just want show up for work, do the least amount of work possible, get a pay check, and then go home. In my view, it's best for everyone if this kind of person went to do something different. (Don't waste your time or energy on them.)

<u>Your Leadership will take on a New Level of POWER because of its Simplicity, Clarity, Your Asking of Questions (and Hearing the Answers) and using Time to Maximize Your Business' Effectiveness.</u>

A Better Way
To Solve Tax Office Problems

When leading your tax business (especially as you prepare for your busiest season), helping solve problems on a daily basis can become very time consuming. Too often, employees bring their problems to the leader (YOU). And for the most part, the owner usually allows himself or herself to be interrupted to help solve whatever the problem is. But I'm here to tell you ... there's a better way!

Let me start out by saying this first: **If you immediately accept responsibility for helping your employees solve their problems, you're doing them a disservice.** They will never grow into the person you want them to be representing your tax business. Stop being your employees' first line of defense. Your tax office will run much more smoothly with fewer problems and hassles IF you allow your staff to take responsibility FIRST for solving whatever issues arise.

BLOCKBUSTER
How To Build A Million Dollar Tax Business

Give your staff an avenue to solve their own problems when they occur without having to get you or anyone else in your office involved. It will take time in the beginning, but in the long run, this investment of giving your employees the gift of personal responsibility will pay you and your tax business back in spades!

You may not realize how valuable your time is, but the more you allow yourself to get interrupted in daily problem-solving activities, the more profit goes down the drain. Oh, you don't think it's a big deal at first. And in some cases, you actually like the attention; it makes you feel important. But these kinds of inner-office operational activities kill your net, and the time lost in opportunity costs can be even more devastating.

So after seeing this problem happen in our tax business for a couple of years, I decided to put a process in place to stop all the unnecessary interruptions of our key employees or managers running the day-to-day operations. Too many employees were not thinking for themselves!

So I devised a short, simple, one-page form. We required that anytime an employee had a question or a problem needing to be solved, they had to fill out this form and bring it to their immediate supervisor or manager in charge of the office.

If it was related to tax preparation, or something having to do with a procedure, or something got misplaced, or whatever the issue was (it didn't matter), we wanted to require the employee to try and figure it out for themselves first.

Here are the questions:

- Define the problem.
- What are possible solutions?
- What's the best way you think the problem could be solved?
- How can you make this solution happen?
- Are there any additional resources you need to solve this problem faster in the future?

Now, there are several things happening all at the same time when you require your employees to jump through a "hoop" like this.

First, just getting someone to define the issue and answer a few pertinent questions is actually healthy. Once they write it out, many times they'll get an answer to fix the problem pretty fast.

Second, employees figure out quickly that they're responsible. They need to try and solve whatever is causing them not to be able to move forward in their job. The good ones like this and will do whatever is needed to get better. The bad employees get frustrated and quit. (This is a good thing. Better to have this happen earlier rather than later.)

Overall, once you first begin implementing this procedure, your employees will push back a little. They will say, "Why do I have to fill out some form? I just have a simple question." You'll say, "Great! Solve your simple question yourself."

Then they figure out that if they have to go through a process of filling out a form every time they have a question, they are better off spending that same time and energy trying to find the answer to their question themselves.

(Exactly ... That's The Whole Point!)

Your Office Processes Will Improve

If your tax business is weak on Systems, the questions your employees raise will act as a flashlight illuminating many of the areas where you need to be more specific in your processes. And if you do have these procedures in place, then you're not doing a good job teaching them (which will help you get better in this area as well).

Either way, <u>more personal responsibility is being taken by you and your staff for the overall effectiveness of your office flow</u>.

And if you keep getting better, the experience your clients receive will be better – which means your tax business is taking steps to reach the next level of success.

Goals

Leaders have goals. The best leaders are excellent at seeing what needs to be achieved and getting people to help them get those desired results.

Obviously, goals are important. <u>But being able to follow clearly defined action steps in order to reach those goals is where the money is</u>. **Most folks don't achieve their goals because they do not simplify, and then perform the actions needed on a daily basis.**

Quality leaders mentor people best by helping them focus on what's important. Getting employees unstuck from side issues and locked in on the task at hand gets the team closer towards the desired goal.

The main reason tax preparers and office staff don't reach their goals is because they spend their time working on the wrong stuff. Great leaders re-focus them on what they agreed to do and give them the tools and encouragement to keep going.

As you lead your employees, whether it's tax season or not, make sure each person has allotted specific time blocks in their daily and weekly schedule to accomplish the tasks related to reaching the goals you've set for your tax office.

A goal is measureable and has a completion date. For extra motivation, write down the reasons why you want to accomplish these goals. For your tax practice, set goals for the person answering the phone. Same with the tax preparer. Don't forget about the back office processors or people helping with administration. Everyone needs clear goals to work towards. And remember, all employee goals are just subset goals leading to your overall tax business goals. (Make sure they are in sync!)

Where The Rubber Meets The Road

Work toward your goals. As the leader, you must actively review and uncover insights about each employee while they work these action steps leading towards the goals. You'll need to document what's going well and what's not going so well with each person. Then as all good leaders do, adjust accordingly.

This is where most employees (and the owner when he or she is trying to help) get stuck. Few people are willing to track the results. If you skip this step, how can you get better the following week? That means on a weekly basis, each goal must have some kind of current status. You're working it. It's a living, breathing goal. There's seven days between here and there. Every couple of days, you're checking the status of how everything is going. What's working? What's not working so well? How can we do something differently to get a better result?

If you're consistently not hitting your goals, or you're not able to work these goals well and see what you're doing right or wrong, chances are there's probably a lack of passion somewhere.

You better be passionate about what you're doing. You must have a real desire to get better and to help the people around you improve. The energy that comes from this passion will help carry you through the times when you don't feel like doing your job that day. Sometimes, just showing up and sticking with it allows you to win!

If your tax business doesn't achieve the goals you set out to accomplish, chances are the majority of the people in your office were not working on the steps needed to reach these goals on a daily basis. And if that's the case, as a leader you must look in the mirror and be honest about what happened, and then go do a better job in your leadership role.

Successful leaders get results by building people and growing them up in their area of giftedness. People will respond to you because they are starved for quality leadership. Again, there's such a lack of good leadership in the tax industry. Once you grow in this area, quality tax pros will flock to your business and want to work with you.

Be great at your leadership. Build people up and help them move forward in their God-given talents. They will be excited and serve your clients with passion. They will work as a team and your clients will notice the difference. They will comment on the "feeling" in your office when they walk in the building. They will hear it in the voices answering the phone. The communication coming from your office (written and verbal) will set you apart. Leadership affects so many different areas of your tax business.

So keep working on yourself as a leader.

You are a great investment for your tax business and the community around you!

Chapter 10

The Tax Biz Millionaire Mindset

This is a significant topic and it deserves a whole seminar in and of itself, but I'm going to try to cover some highlights in this chapter to better equip you to make more money because tax professionals with a million-dollar mindset really do have an advantage over their competition.

As the owner of a tax business, you are either attracting money, deal flow and wealth opportunities, or you are repelling them. Making significant sums of money sounds good on the outside, but when you begin to get down to brass tacks, some have a tendency to push wealth-producing business opportunities away without even realizing it.

Is it possible that you could feel uncomfortable receiving a big deal if the opportunity crossed your desk? You've always said you'd love the right situation to come up for your tax business to add a bunch of extra zeros at the end of the regular income number your tax business normally makes each year.

Maybe you feel a little uneasy, and you sabotage yourself when sitting with a potential client whose small business account would normally be worth $2,500 to $3,000 per year – but the vibe you portray when discussing $25,000 or $30,000 on a similar small business account is overwhelming to you. In turn, that potential client gets cold feet and the deal is off.

BLOCKBUSTER
How To Build A Million Dollar Tax Business

Personally, I've always had a larger-than-life mindset. The sky is the limit. The larger the deal, the more excited I get. However, I understand that other business owners do experience various levels of discomfort. I coached a tax business owner who felt completely fine with a chance to earn an extra $100,000 on a deal. No problem. But that same coaching client, when presented with the opportunity to grow to a $5 Million Dollar Company could not even imagine it. I even ran the numbers for him, sharing the business plan scenarios in a couple different ways. It was like his brain went blank. His mindset for himself and his tax business could not get there.

We've all had good and bad thoughts about ourselves growing up. What comments did we overhear from the top of the staircase in our youth? Did our parents tell us we couldn't do a particular thing during our teenage years? Or did a teacher or coach encourage us beyond our wildest dreams?

Back when you first got into the tax business, were you completely confident, or did you experience doubting voices in the back of your brain? Many tax professionals have those doubting thoughts come into their minds at certain pivotal moments during important deals.

Any time I ever have little whispers of negative voices coming into my thought process, I pretty much tell them to take a hike. I just say no to whatever bad scenario that is last in my mind: I say to go jump in a lake. Then I'll think or on occasion speak the opposite over my life and my mind immediately afterwards.

Seriously, everyone has negative or self-defeating thoughts every now and then. The issue is, what do you do with them? Well, you can believe them, or you can recognize that they're not true and dismiss them. Your choice.

Attract Money

Not being in touch with how money flows will actually have a negative impact on your tax business's bottom line. Honestly, money flows to you when you expect it. Wealth presents itself when you accept additional deal flow as a good thing.

Now, foolish people think that just hoping for more money works to increase your wealth. Right-thinking, wealth-minded people plan for it. They set their businesses up in a systematic way to handle it. They build wealth by not letting a day go by without running some kind of ad or promotion to tap into a new revenue stream. With everything a wealth-attraction business person does each day, they have a healthy expectation of seeing money flowing their way.

No Entitlement Zone

Money does not flow your way when you feel entitled to it. An entitlement attitude is poisonous. If you think you're supposed to have something because you have a few letters behind your name, that mindset will destroy your tax business.

Clarity

Right thinking begins with clarifying to yourself who you are and what you're all about. You must have a governing philosophy that heads your decision making process. This mindset brings a real strong sense of self and increases your confidence level in all that you do. When you engage other people from a personal standpoint, they'll notice quickly that you live your life without distraction. Whatever conversation you are in, whether it's in-person, by email or over the phone, when you know who you are and what you're all about, you don't have to articulate an "official" philosophy. It just comes out in how you talk with people. How you say "yes" and how you say "no" speaks volumes. Over time, the **personal clarity** on your life will break through the clutter of everyone else's lives around you, allowing money to flow your way.

Another way money flows in your direction is when you enjoy **client clarity**. You'll have laser like focus on who you're for, and who you're not for from a target marketing standpoint. Who do you and your tax business appeal to the most? Who's best matched to do business with you? *Authenticity* is very powerful. So when you speak from your heart to this targeted people group, they follow and do everything you have to say. Once you've built relationship with this type of client, they will climb a mountain for you. Your advocacy for them is powerful and actually draws more of these kinds of clients to you. And of course, these clients will buy what you recommend, leading to the generation of more wealth.

Money Insight: <u>Wealth is facilitated by a specific audience. So if you build your tax business by narrowing your focus, you actually will get more business</u>. Most tax professionals think the opposite. In their mind, "everyone has to file a tax return, which means everyone is my potential client." Wrong. That's bad thinking, because if everyone is your client, then no one is your client. (You just can't be all things to all people – it's not possible.)

Think niche.

Focus on a niche group or groups. Build your tax business by narrowing your focus. Instead of advertising your tax practice to an ocean, promote yourself as the big fish in four or five niche-specific small ponds. THIS IS WHERE THE MONEY FLOWS.

Marketing message clarity. You've got to differentiate or you'll die. You've got to be different or you'll be out of business. The tax industry is so commoditized, that if you don't set yourself apart, you're in big trouble. That's why it's so important to articulate in your marketing why you are FOR THEM (your potential target client). Why should your target market listen to you right now? This type of communication is market message clarity at its best.

When your tax business communicates your Personal Clarity, Client Clarity and Market Message Clarity – ALL AT THE SAME TIME – your life will align with your tax business, which, in turn, will open the door for increased revenue flow into your bank account.

Let me give you a quote from *Secret of the Ages*, a book by Robert Collier.

It's about the power of real focus and concentration.

"The answer is simply that you have never focused your desires into one great dominating desire or objective. You have a host of mild desires. You mildly wish you're rich. You mildly wish you have a position of a responsibility and influence. You wish you were free to travel at will. The wishes are so many and varied that they conflict with each other. They confuse and you get nowhere in particular. You lack one intense desire to the accomplishment of which you are willing to subordinate everything else."

Just as Robert Collier says, most tax business owners wish this, or they wish that. They hope for this, or they hope for that. There's little clarity and focus (if any) on the actions required towards reaching the goals that dominate their desires. The other smaller issues get in the way so they kind of wander around in the same old pattern, doing the same old stuff they always do in their tax practice. Something needs to change here!

Congruency

This chapter is about a tax business owner's millionaire mindset, right? What you think about has to be congruent with your actions. This is not positive thinking. I'm a huge fan of positive thinking, but you don't get anywhere in life and running a successful business with positive thinking alone.

You must do the work. Get in motion by taking action. Then focus on proper action. (Doing the right things.) Then, purposefully, these action steps need to be taken strategically. (You have a reason behind the order of your actions.) And all of these steps forward are bathed with a positive mental attitude.

But here's the deal. Ninety percent or more of goals are not that difficult to achieve. The main reason goals are not reached: THE ACTIONS TAKEN ON A DAILY BASIS ARE NOT CONGRUENT WITH THE GOALS.

Most tax professionals do not have specific goals written down with a deadline date. So if that's you, start there. But once you've completed the written goals part of the equation, next comes the part which separates the wannabees and the true go-getters.

Real world wealth is attracted to those who organize their actions and follow a behavior pattern required to achieve those stated goals. So writing down the goals is not enough. Anybody can do that. In addition, document the behavior congruent with reaching your goals. By taking these purposeful action steps over a specific period of time (with a real deadline) you will achieve your goals.

Attach Time in Your Schedule for Each Important Step.

Monitor benchmarks so you finish what needs to be accomplished by the deadline date. As you repeat this process you are consistently moving "the ball" forward to the goal line.

Wisdom Insight

When you're executing your goals, you'll want to ask and answer these questions along the way:

- <u>Is this use of my time (what I'm doing right now) moving me measurably closer to my goals?</u>

- <u>Is this use of my money (whatever I happen to be investing in right now) moving me measurably closer to my goals?</u>

If not, why am I doing it?

If you LIVE OUT this one wisdom insight I just wrote, it will absolutely change your life.

Keep in mind, because you don't live in a bubble, there are other people around you who'll try and impact your life in a not-so-good-way. Life happens and bad things do occur all the time in the real world. Relationships with people close to you can get messy. And I can tell you from plenty of personal experience, many people you come in contact with will NEVER have any serious plans to pursue their goals or live out the dream deep in their heart. (If they did, everyone would be successful.)

Mike Murdock says it better in the *Secrets of the Richest Man Who Ever Lived (The Life of King Solomon.)*

"Few people around you have any serious plans they are pursuing on a daily basis."

This means when you're serious about your life and you're pursuing your goals and you desire to grow and get better in everything you put your hands to, other people aren't going to like it. Many of your friends and associates actually are going to be offended by your pursuit to be more successful. The truth is, some will try to sabotage you because they don't like the fact that you're doing something that has meaning and purpose ... while they look at their lives and realize they're not really doing anything worth a darn.

You must stay strong when those around you don't believe in you. It's best to find a few comrades you can "walk through life with" and encourage one another. Pick one another up when one of you is feeling down. It could be close friends or business associates in or out of town. Or even your spouse.

Don't expect people to cheer you on when you get to the top. As a mentor once told me, "It's lonely up here. Get used to it because few people ever make it this high."

Opinions Don't Matter

Oh, and if you didn't realize, other people are going to have an opinion about what you're doing. Most of these opinions are completely off because, number one, these people have their own baggage, and number two, they lack access to the full picture of what you are doing.

The last thing you need to do is believe what other people are saying about you. Most of the people who give you their opinion (about running a success business etc) are not qualified to give you an informed opinion anyway. If you actually take the time to entertain the ideas coming from these unqualified people, you can destroy your business pretty quick.

Stay focused on your plan. Other people are going to say things about you and do things to you that can cause you to get off track. DON'T LET THIS HAPPEN.

Tax Industry Example:

Let me give you a common example inside the tax industry where almost everyone is wrong. Here it is ... wait for it ... "Increasing my prices is going to hurt my business."

Well, having been a marketing consultant and business growth coach to the tax industry for a couple of decades (helping thousands of independent tax business owners) and owning my own tax business where we tested this strategy for 10 straight years ... I'm qualified to say: the exact opposite is true.

Increasing your prices is going to greatly help your business. Just do the math. I'm not going to explain all the reasons why here (see other chapters in this book). But hundreds of thousands of tax professionals in the United States actually think to be more successful, it's best to offer low prices on their tax services.

Another Important Tax Industry Example:

Tax professionals think they must service a high volume of clients to make seven-figure money. This is not true. Just look at the following unique way to profit from the IRS Resolution Business.

www.MillionDollarTaxBiz.com/IRSHelpBiz

Let me quote Stuart Wilde:

"To make a lot of money, you have to decide to be abnormal, to become a truly independent being."

Most people don't make a lot of money because they're not willing to be abnormal.

They just want to be regular like everybody else. But truly successful people have an inner drive. They're moving forward. They're doing things that other people aren't willing to take the time to do, and that's what sets them apart, getting them ahead of the crowd.

Tax business owners who attract high levels of wealth have a very high immunity to criticism. Since I've given you advanced warning, you might as well begin growing some thick skin now. Successful tax pros aren't in the business of seeking other people's approval. They just don't have the time to be worrying about what other people think.

FINAL WARNING:

Almost everyone around you will resent your ambitions for independence and living your life successfully on your terms. They will even consciously or unconsciously undermine your efforts. Some will try to sabotage you. They want to disrupt your plans. That's why they are criticizing you. Some will even try to make you feel guilty about your accomplishments and your achievements. Then, when all else fails, those "little people" (drunk with jealousy) will seek to impose new rules and regulations on you with the hope they can help destroy everything you've worked so hard for.

But hey, this is the life of a successful entrepreneur.

The benefits are worth it! When you climb high up on that success ladder, you expose yourself more and people take shots at you. Just get used to it.

As the old saying goes, if it's too hot in the kitchen, and you're unwilling to take the heat – time to get out of the kitchen and do something else.

Wealth attraction and the millionaire mindset are for the bold. Be bold.

Have bold ideas. Make bold plans. Live a bold mission. Promise bold guarantees.

One of the biggest differences between successful tax businesses and tax pros barely making it from year-to-year is the sense of urgency.

Make your plans and get them done. Start doing it – now.

"Your Ship" Will Come In

What's your response time for implementing a big opportunity in your business?

The shorter the distance between when you get a great idea and when you implement it, the more success you will achieve.

Remember, your ship can't come in unless you have first sent it out.

Everybody wants their ship to come in, but most people aren't taking the necessary steps to market themselves and consistently send ships out on a daily basis.

BLOCKBUSTER
How To Build A Million Dollar Tax Business

Note to Self:

Decide to send out a few quality ships this week, this month ... and I promise, a few very nice profitable opportunity ships will come back in for you.

Lastly, I'll say this:

Attach the right money-making mindset to the right wealth-producing success tools and you'll have massive success on your hands. Having the right mindset really does start behind your eyes.

At the end of the day, once you are mentally ready, you'll put the pieces together to get your tax business to the million-dollar level.

Chapter 11

Finally! Achieving Your Tax Biz Dreams

Reaching your tax business' goals and finally achieving the results that you've always dreamed of is what every tax business owner wants.

Back when we had just one tax office, I dreamed of running a much larger multi-location tax business enterprise. I decided way back then that we were going to work harder, work faster and work smarter than our competition.

We were going to do things that our competition wasn't willing to do. I was extremely competitive, and I was determined to beat our competition.

Translation:

After April 15, when many tax professionals took their foot off the gas pedal and slowed down on their work schedule in the off season, we shifted into a higher gear and used this time to get better at growing our tax business organization.

Of course, everybody has a higher speed during tax season, but we decided one of the ways to get ahead of our competition was to outwork them in the offseason. A couple weeks after the IRS deadline, we were locked into serious strategic planning mode. In May each year, we started a process to develop a clear plan for the next eight months. This included measurable goals, specific action steps to reach these goals, timelines assigned in our project calendar and a person's name attached to each project for accountability. So when tax season came around again, we'd move ahead of our competition more and more each year.

Now, that didn't mean we didn't take time off in the summer, go on vacation and play at the pool with our kids. We did tone down the project workload from June 15 to August 15 and took advantage of having an offseason in our industry. But we (my leadership team and I) were busier in the fall getting ready for tax season than we were in tax season itself.

During tax season, I always hired other qualified employees to do the work of running the day-to-day operations of our tax business. If I was going to lead our company well, I knew I could not get involved in the actual workflow of the organization.

I purposefully chose to work ON the business, not IN the business, to better help us achieve our goals and reach our dreams of running a very successful multi-location tax firm.

The Annual Cycle Of Your Tax Business

Let me give you a little more detail on the successful rhythm of our tax business. During tax season I was an encourager. I'd build up my employees and managers while they worked hard taking care of clients. Yes, I brought "the hammer" by being the person who had to make tough decisions for accountability purposes. But all in all, I did my best to make sure quality employees had what they needed, and then I got out of the way.

Like I said earlier, we did our strategic planning in the offseason. After April 15, those who worked hard in the tax offices took a break until the end of the month. Then from basically May 1 through June 15, we worked hard at figuring out everything that we were doing right, everything that we were doing wrong, and all the different changes and upgrades we needed to do. These lists were then prioritized and added to a timeline on a calendar. If we waited until the summer or fall to do this kind of work, we'd miss something. While everything was still fresh in our minds, we collected all the employees' feedback and then we hashed through what would be best and what tools and resources were needed to get the job done.

The work schedule was much lighter from mid-June to mid-August when kids started to go back to school. The key was, before everyone "checked out" after June 15, they had a clear, doable work schedule – week by week (usually with at least one other person for accountability) so everything was completed when needed before a busier fall schedule came around.

Timelines and projects were laid out. Certain tasks came first, second, third, etc., with deadlines and follow-up to make sure each project was completed correctly.

Year after year, we improved as a company.

Good Idea, 5 Percent ...
Execution, 95 Percent

Good ideas are a dime a dozen. Good ideas don't make businesses great. Now don't get me wrong, you want really good ideas to help you move in the right direction and make you better. But good ideas are only five percent of the equation.

Ninety-five percent of running the successful business you've always dreamed of is on the execution side. The next time you are in a business meeting, don't spend the majority of your time trying to come up with good ideas. Figure out your top three objectives and then spend MOST of your time and energy on implementing those good ideas successfully.

Communication

After several years of seeing significant improvement in almost every area of our tax business, we started to level off. When tax season came, our execution was lacking. We were not hitting most of our goals in the same way we were before. And as the leader, I was at a loss. What was the problem?

Then one day it hit me.

WE WERE NOT COMMUNICATING WELL.

We had no organized process (system) for HOW we communicated within our company.

It was my job to make sure everyone was receiving proper communication in multiple different formats. I needed to ensure all my employees were crystal clear on what we were doing, why we were doing it, and the expectations involved in making whatever we were doing a success. You might think this doesn't sound like that big of a deal. But it was a huge step forward in our organization, and we saw better results immediately once we better formalized our communication processes.

Lack of Accountability

One of the hidden problems we found was a lack of accountability on the front line of our tax business. Let me say it straight: **if you want to achieve your dreams in**

your tax business, you better have a significant focus on accountability. I'm talking about for you personally and also your business. You will make great strides as the owner if you formalize some kind of accountability structure for yourself. In addition, some type of rewards-and-consequences system must be embedded into the fabric of your business as well.

If you want to take your tax business to the next level of success, there must be consequences and rewards for all of the important projects you're working on – daily, weekly and on a monthly basis.

When I talk about accountability in the seminar room, most times I'll see eyes glaze over. Tax pros don't always want to hear this. However, to people who are living their dreams and achieving their goals and ultimately enjoying the fruits of their labor, accountability is high on their priority list.

Wisdom

You've got to have wisdom when deciding how you spend your time. If you're going to achieve the dreams you have for your life, you want to be very careful about what you agree to. Opportunities are everywhere. But you only have so much time, and the time you do have must be viewed through the window of your purposed lifestyle desires.

Wisdom says you're only one person and you can only do so much. You must have a plan related to how you'll spend your minutes, your hours and each of your days.

The same holds true with your opportunities. There are some opportunities that are really good, but they don't fit in with what you say is important with your business and your lifestyle choices. By the same token, when other opportunities pop up, they completely align with what you're trying to do, so it's easy for you to say yes.

Let's touch on the lifestyle issue real quick.

You're doing all of this work in and through your business for a better lifestyle, right? (Lifestyle might not be THE reason, but it's pretty high up on most people's list.) You're working hard now so you don't have to live a stressed-out life later. It's good to have seasons of hard work, as long as you have extended seasons of breaks, too.

Remember, you're building your business so you can enjoy your time building relationships with the people you love. You don't want to make business an idol so you have no life outside of work. Some tax professionals don't realize that they have no life until they look around and notice they have no outside activities other than work. Soon owners understand they must better balance the way they're living their life. Don't wait until a personal crisis pops up in your life to restructure some of your lifestyle and business commitments.

I recommend you make the changes best for your life – now.

Activity
vs.
Accomplishment

During tax season especially, I've noticed tax professionals love to be active, but in their busyness they don't accomplish as much as they think they do.

<u>If you could do nothing else, but cut activity disguised as accomplishment by 50 percent, your profits would skyrocket and you'd have all the time you needed to do the things you say you want to get done in your business.</u>

Activity is easy to recognize. Just look at the normal routine in your office. The busyness when the phone rings or when the clients walk in, or whatever projects you're working on. During tax season, you can have twenty things on your to-do list each day and most times, only two or three items are completed. Why? Because when you walked in your office, all hell breaks loose. Everyone wants a piece of you, the office equipment doesn't work, some technology procedure is messed up, and your clients are mad because (pick a number), and that file is missing, and blah, blah, blah.

Now let's look at the good side of increased activity.

There are many clients coming into your office. All the technology is working right, and all your clients are being taken care of well. Your employees are working smart and you're feeling good about the flow of your office. As the owner, you're walking around answering questions and helping solve problems. Employees are taking care of the immediate tasks on their plate and basically, everyone in the office seems to be doing what they are supposed to do during tax season. There's a lot of activity … **BUT how much of that activity is accomplishment and leading you closer towards your goals?**

Accomplishment is getting the right things done. <u>Accomplishment always describes your priorities in the past tense.</u>

Highest level accomplishment can immediately be linked to profit margin or tracked as directly contributing to your stated goals.

This is key.

<u>Accomplishment is getting stuff done that actually gets you closer to your goals or what you say is important to your tax business.</u>

Tax business owners set goals for tax season. Some will even write these goals down on paper. Better yet, you might even take each goal and add three to five action steps detailing what must happen to achieve each goal.

But the problem is, when tax season comes, you spend your time (or your employees' time) in increased activity instead of "working your goals," which doesn't match with what you said you needed to do to be successful in your tax business.

Accomplishment is what leads you to your dreams.

It's what successful people thrive on. As the owner, you must accomplish what you say is important and delegate or dump the other activities that aren't as important.

The Secret Sauce for Success

If you truly want to move to the head of the line professionally (or in any area of your life) then follow this Simple Four-Step Formula. **There are ONLY Four Steps!**

Step #1

Decide what you want to get done today.

Step #2

Assign each project a specific block of time.

Step #3

Script your day in 15-minute to hourly time blocks in priority order.

Step #4

Bar all distractions and interruptions until you're done.

What I just said is very simple, but very hard to do. But if you work at this simple formula every day, its impact on your life will be a game-changer. You say you want to reach your dreams ... so DO these four steps.

This formula is the secret sauce for success. You don't need a bunch of fantasy computer technologies or smart phone gizmos or the next greatest celebrity brand or whatever else someone told you was needed for success.

What I'm talking about is **self-governance.** (This is not time management.)

This is about you, the owner, starting your day knowing the important things that must get done for you to be more successful. You do not make a to-do list. You make a DONE list. Decide what will get done today – and do it. (There is a huge difference here.)

To maximize effectiveness, you must assign blocks of time to whatever is on your Done List each day. It might be fifteen minutes or three hours, but you allot a measurable time frame. If it's three hours, you'll probably need to break down the project into smaller chunks. (Like one hour for the first third of the project.) The smaller the amount of time, the better you will be at holding yourself accountable.

From my experience, if you've not completed projects like this before, it'll take you a couple of months to develop this ability. Forcing yourself to get things done (no matter what comes up each day) is a skill learned only from experience.

After a few weeks, you'll realize how little you know about how much time it actually takes to complete a variety of tasks. Since you've never tracked your time so rigorously, you'll be surprised at how long things take. Like everyone else, you'll need to expand your time frame for completely finishing tasks until you teach yourself to work faster. (Again, being efficient is a skill you can improve on.)

One of the top benefits of completing your Done List on a daily basis is that the "not-so-important-stuff" piles up, and forces you to delegate it. Either someone in your office gets additional work put on their plate, or you hire a part-time administration person to handle these details so nothing falls through the cracks. Once you realize you can meet with this person for ten minutes, three times per day (early in the morning, middle of the day around lunch, and then late afternoon to confirm what did or didn't get finalized that day), you'll be thrilled to gain about fifteen or twenty hours of your week back! (Notice only thirty minutes total investment of your time, five days per week.)

I can't tell you how good it feels when you're actually getting DONE what you know is very important for your business' success, ON TIME, every day you go to your office. These four steps work so well that (like me) you'll want to introduce a "softer" version of this success formula for your personal life.

Scheduling Productivity At Best And Worst Times

If you really want to get something done (and done well), it just makes sense to block off time to do it when you are most productive. If you are a morning person, you'll work on your most important projects in the morning. If you are an evening person, then give yourself a couple of extra evenings to complete whatever projects you have on your Done List. Routinely add your top priorities to your calendar at your peak productive times and you'll triple your effectiveness moving forward.

Conversely, we all have "things" that only we can do, but aren't very important. You'll need to bundle these details into one of your worst productive times during your work week. I have two categories. Stuff I need to deal with in the current week. (I have two hours blocked at the end of every week.) And then I take one full day every month to do nothing but the things that can wait, but aren't going to be delegated to an assistant.

It really is important for you to plan and schedule these kinds of less important items, because, you know you'll get to it when the time comes, and this frees up your mind to stay focused on the current tasks at hand.

Time Sucking Vampires

The biggest time-sucking problems you'll face relate to people. Your employees, clients, friends, family or even business peers can act like vampires and suck the time right out of your schedule. However, **time vampires only suck your time away IF you let them.**

As the owner, you'll have to set some clear working boundaries around you. These will be your no-interruption zones: certain blocks of time in your day, and during every week, where no one bothers you.

<u>No Phones, No Email, No Texting, No People ...</u>
<u>No Nothing Except The High Priority Project</u>
<u>You're Getting Done That Day.</u>
<u>I Don't Care If Your Office Is On Fire.</u>
<u>No Interruptions.</u>

BLOCKBUSTER
How To Build A Million Dollar Tax Business

Remember, these blocked-off, no-interruption zones are not all the time. You actually want to build time into each day when your staff can come and ask you questions. These hours are for mentoring and investing in them. (They get your full attention.) Bundle as much training and upgrading of your processes as you can here.

I also recommend you bundle your correspondence into a couple time-blocked windows each week. Make your outbound calls, schedule your phone appointments and compose the letters you need for written communication – but do so at specific assigned times.

Email can be daily, but limited to three short blocks of time (Early, Middle, Late).

And if you're someone who dabbles in social media during your work day ... Quit.

Save it for the end of the day at home – or at worst, twenty minutes while you eat lunch. If you can't do this, I'd consider unplugging all together until you can control your addiction.

I hope all of this is making sense. Some tax business owners will take what I'm saying the wrong way.

My advice to you:

Do whatever version of massive productivity you want, but don't come back to me and complain how you never get anything done in your business. Either jump on board with my advice or make your own self-governance work for you.

BLOCKBUSTER
How To Build A Million Dollar Tax Business

Living The Dream

If you're going to live your dream, you must gain "clarity of purpose" on what you really want to do and why you're willing to do whatever it takes to get there.

What I'm about to say now needs to be written down. So pull out your separate piece of paper again.

Answer these questions now, if possible.

- What do you really want out of your tax business? (Benefits)

- What are you willing to do to implement the business results you need?

- Are you satisfied with the current results in your business? What will you do different?

- Do you think you can improve your tax business? In what areas? How?

- What are the biggest factors holding you back from achieving what you say you want out of business?

- What are your personal obstacles?

For each obstacle, what three things can you do to overcome that obstacle in the next twenty-one days?

After twenty-one days, re-evaluate, update your list and repeat.

Now, if these obstacles were eliminated and the problems in your tax business were gone (in the next six to eighteen months), what are the benefits you'd experience as a result?

Here's the Million-Dollar Question:

Do these benefits match with what you want from your tax business?

(see the first question)

I want you to be honest. If you overcame your obstacles in six to eighteen months and you get the benefits that you said you wanted, do they match up with the first question I asked you?

If your answers aren't matching, you need to change something.

How motivated are you to do whatever it takes to get what you want most out of your business?

If you're willing to take systematic and purposeful action towards breaking down the barriers that have been holding back your success, but your answers are not matching with what you originally said you wanted out of your business, then ...

Re-think and submit your answers so that WHAT YOU SAY YOU WANT is in alignment with WHAT YOU'RE WILLING TO DO -- starting today!

Hopefully, this little exercise brought some new insight into how to overcome your obstacles, so you can be more successful in your personal and business life.

BLOCKBUSTER
How To Build A Million Dollar Tax Business

If you believe you can take personal responsibility for solving the issues in your life and follow a consistent plan aligned with the benefits you want most from your tax business – you WILL achieve your dreams!

Chapter 12

For Tax Business Owners: The Opportunity Of Our Lifetime

Obamacare or The Affordable Care Act (ACA) is a significant piece of legislation impacting our nation. And I'm not going to get into whether I like it or dislike it. (Not the point of this chapter.) I've put on my marketing, consulting and tax-business-success-coaching hat and I'm asking the question for my tax business owner clients, "How are you making more money as a result of ACA?"

You are in business to keep the IRS off people's backs. This is what you do to earn a living. The Healthcare Industry, plus the Health and Human Services Department, injected itself into the tax industry, which impacts your livelihood.

Again, I'm not talking about whether you like Obamacare or dislike Obamacare.

But Healthcare and Taxes are now joined at the hip forever, like it or not.

What are you doing to not only protect yourself, but also to increase your revenue from all the new regulations you're required to know and help your clients with?

Okay, let me back up a bit.

BLOCKBUSTER
How To Build A Million Dollar Tax Business

The ACA legislation was signed into law, March 23, 2010. The Supreme Court called Obamacare a "tax" on June 28, 2012. This law empowers the IRS to enforce ACA compliance, which definitely impacts you as a tax professional. And now, everyone in the tax industry must combine and provide ACA reporting as part of their tax filing services. Then the Supreme Court (again) ruled in favor of Obamacare on June 25, 2015.

Obamacare has been a law for a number of years now. And this <u>historical shift impacting the tax industry could be the greatest opportunity to create wealth for a tax business in our lifetime.</u>

Now, that's a big statement. But hear me out.

Currently, Healthcare accounts for almost one-fifth of the United States' economy (about twenty cents for every dollar circulating in our nation.) And as I've just stated, healthcare and filing tax returns are now legally bound together. That means from here on out, there'll be significant chunks of healthcare dollars moving into the tax industry. (And this percentage will only increase as each year passes.)

Money moves and shifts directions through our economy all the time. Wealth needs a place to go. Right now, there is a great opportunity for tax professionals to stake claim in what I see as a new ACA Gold Rush.

As a tax professional, you're committed to making your tax business better. Meaning, if there are additional revenue streams available for savvy tax pros, you'd be interested in tapping into them.

If you had high-net-worth individuals coming to you for ACA advice, I'm sure you'd be open to helping them and getting paid for it, right? If you could offer additional profit-producing services in your tax practice (not just during tax season, but year-round) you'd be willing to participate, right? If you could be the go-to tax professional helping middle income taxpayers in your city with not only taxes, but insurance-related services – that would be alright with you as long as you're getting paid, right?

Taxes, health insurance and other financial services are all on a collision course with taxpayers needing professional help. Year-round audit and compliance services will be one of the main new emerging businesses for the ACA tax professional.

For the tax pros who are early adopters, this new revenue source will eventually dwarf their current seasonal tax practice.

And yes, **this Healthcare and Tax Collision will get complicated. But, the bigger the problem, the bigger the reward.**

And the ACA will be a huge problem not only for taxpayers who pay a professional to help them file their taxes each year, but also in my eyes, for taxpayers who normally prepare their own return. Most of them will require help navigating these rough waters of ACA implementation. Health and Human Services, partnered with the IRS, are just not set up to handle the size and scope of these changes impacting the tax filing landscape.

Good or bad, the problems will land back in the local tax professional's lap. Where else will a taxpayer go for professional help? The owner of a tax practice is on the front line and is the most natural place for a person with a tax filing issue to go.

<u>If you plan on staying in the tax industry, you won't have a choice. You'll have to deal with ACA. Might as well cash in on this river of new revenue flowing your way.</u>

BLOCKBUSTER
How To Build A Million Dollar Tax Business

Whether you like it or not, the IRS is turning the tax profession into their compliance department. You will have to audit not only your tax client's Health Insurance and Tax regulation paperwork in the off season, but also any new client when they call or walk into your office. Charging additional fees will be mandatory.

Back in the late 1980's when electronic filing was first introduced into the tax industry, there were early adapters. Many tax professionals increased their revenue in many different ways based on their personal preference and the business model they were comfortable with. Several other financial industries jumped in and got involved with the tax industry when the refund anticipation loan became popular with lower income folks.

A huge niche within the tax industry was formed and significant wealth was achieved by many. Thirty or more years later, it matured like every industry does. The opportunities are fewer and the landscape is much different now.

The Affordable Care Act (Obamacare) will have a greater impact on the tax industry because of the link with health insurance on the tax return. Once Obamacare was officially labeled a tax, all Americans would eventually be impacted.

That means new businesses, new ventures, new departments and new industries will all migrate to the tax industry. Why? Because that's where the money is flowing.

Whatever services you offer in your tax practice, I guarantee you'll be forced to upgrade or change these services because of the ACA legislation requirements.

When opportunities arise, the businesses with the best marketing win.

As a tax pro, what can you do from a marketing perspective to position yourself to get the phone call? Because isn't getting a prospect to call your office the key lever point in this whole thing? If you don't get your phone to ring, how will you be able to take advantage of this opportunity?

Every tax professional wants more new clients. And of course, those same tax pros would like more profit from each client they have now, too.

To get more new clients and to also make more money from your existing clients, you must differentiate yourself. And in this case, the best way to differentiate yourself in today's tax filing marketplace is to focus on The Affordable Care Act in some way.

Perception is everything. In the real world, when people are trying to figure out what to do about filing their taxes, all of the tax professionals look the same. How can they tell you apart from your competition? They can't – unless you help them.

If you are perceived as an *ACA Tax Pro Expert*, you will at least get a call. (And truthfully, that's all good marketing is supposed to do.) This gives you a chance to "sell" them on making an appointment or showing up in your office.

At some point, taxpayers will begin to panic when Obamacare and the IRS are all over the news. The media will do their job and raise awareness. Then word-of-mouth will travel through enough friends and family members complaining about their taxes or health insurance problems. Employers will pass along "new forms" that working folks are not accustomed to seeing. Then the tipping point will come. A certain percentage of the population will get fed up and complain to their elected officials. Social Media will be a tool used to gather masses of disgruntled taxpayers. And, in a few cases, you might even see civil unrest.

However, as tax professional, YOU will be a part of the answer. You'll be wearing the "white hat" and save the day as the local ACA Tax Pro Hero!

For the most up-to-date information on **How Tax Business Owners Can Profit From Obamacare (ACA)**,

I recommend you access this website:

www.MillionDollarTaxBiz.com/ACAExpert

"In The Land Of The Blind, The One-Eyed Man Is King"

This statement had a profound impact on me as I was growing our tax business to the multi-million-dollar level: "In the land of the blind, the one-eyed man is King."

Let me explain.

Sometime around the mid-1990's, our tax business was doing very well. We'd grown to over a million dollars a year and decided to expand from four locations to nine tax offices the following year. Everything was going well. But I wanted our business to be even better; so I decided to get some additional promotional help to ignite our growth even more.

Dan Kennedy was (and still is) one of the best marketing geniuses on the planet. So I decided to write him a big check and pay for a day of his consulting time.

I was going to be vacationing with my wife in Vail, Colorado, and Dan happened to have a speaking gig in

Denver that same week. We worked it out so that on my vacation, I'd spend one of those days with Dan hashing through all my tax business marketing campaigns to improve their results, plus learn some new ways to promote our tax business at the same time.

BLOCKBUSTER
How To Build A Million Dollar Tax Business

Now I must admit, on the marketing side of things, our tax business was doing pretty well. But again, I wanted to get better. However, after spending the morning with a true marketing legend, my eyes were opened to a new level of promotional power. I had one of those "light-bulb-over-my-head" moments. (I mean it.) Everything in an instant just clicked after Dan walked me through a series of sample campaigns for growing each of our tax offices.

Dan Kennedy, in a methodical, step-by-step fashion, revealed to me a more efficient way to market and find quality clients for our tax offices. He shared important financial matrices for growing a business. Plus, Dan revealed how to decide on what and where to spend future marketing dollars. He also helped me understand what to test and how to allocate resources per campaign. Then Dan explained what to expect from my new lead generation ads and how to master the follow-up phases of these promotions.

Everything was so systematic. There was a reason and purpose to every step. I loved it! (I got goosebumps I was so excited.)

So after this revelatory moment, I was sitting there and I said, "Dan, why don't you write all this sales copy for me? I'd like to hire you to prepare all of my marketing campaigns for me." (I knew this would cost a small fortune, but again – it would be worth every penny.)

Then Dan looked at me and said, "Chauncey, you don't need me." And I said, "What do you mean?" He followed up and proclaimed, "In the land of the blind, the one-eyed man is King."

I looked back at him with my head cocked to the side and a quizzical look on my face. I responded, "What? I don't get it. What do you mean?"

BLOCKBUSTER
How To Build A Million Dollar Tax Business

Dan's reply was classic...

"The tax industry is completely blind when it comes to advertising, promotion and marketing their businesses. You can be King (the leader) in your market area with just one eye. You don't need both eyes. Your tax pro competition can't see (do) a thing when it comes to properly growing their business!"

He went on ...

"You don't need to pay me to do all this custom marketing, advertising and sales copy writing for you. Two eyes are not needed to be the top producing tax practice in every city you're in. A one-eyed man IS King if he's competing for tax clients in your kind of marketplace environment."

And here's the punchline.

What Dan Kennedy said about your tax business competition back then is even more true in today's tax industry!

Some of you might be thinking, what if I could hire Chauncey to sit with me for a day and help me just like he got help from Dan Kennedy?

Well, my response would be that's unnecessary, because I've taken almost everything I know about growing a tax business to the million dollar level and put it into an online *Real Tax Business Success Membership System.*

No need to re-invent the wheel.

I show you how to overcome every obstacle in your way so you can take your tax practice to whatever level you so desire.

BLOCKBUSTER
How To Build A Million Dollar Tax Business

<u>I spell everything out in detail from Marketing, Salesmanship, Operations, Recruiting, Hiring, Leadership, Management, Training Employees, Systems and Tracking ... to whatever you need most to run a successful tax business.</u>

Everything is pretty much done for you. All you have to do is just cut and paste, change a few things around and apply it to your business. Then you're off to the races.

You WILL BE the one-eyed King in the land of the blind, in your city where your tax business competition is blind to everything you're doing.

As King, you'll have access to my Done-For-You Tax Business Success System that's got all my most profitable material and all my latest techniques and even the best (fastest) ways to take the stress and headaches out of your life.

I've completely shortened the process for you to get new clients and increase your net income profits better than any other tax pro competitors in your area.

REMEMBER, IN THIS LAND OF THE BLIND, YOU JUST HAVE TO BE A LITTLE BIT BETTER THAN YOUR COMPETITION .... MY MILLION DOLLAR TAX BUSINESS BUILDER SUCCESS SYSTEM IS ALL YOU'LL NEED TO WIN!

Where Real Tax Business Success
Can Happen FOR YOU

www.MillionDollarTaxBiz.com/Membership

Chauncey's Recommended Tax Business Success

RESOURCES

See More Opportunities
ONLINE

www.MillionDollarTaxBizBook.com

Choosing *Drake Software* Was Pivotal To Our Million Dollar Tax Business Success!

Chauncey F. Hutter, Sr.

In 1988, during the early stages of electronic tax filing, I had to make an important choice for my tax business. What tax software should I use?

Turns out, choosing the right tax software was important, but WHO STOOD BEHIND THAT TAX SOFTWARE WAS MORE IMPORTANT.

After watching a short demo in a D.C. airport, a look in their eyes and a handshake ....
I chose DRAKE.

Reflecting back on that important decision many decades later, I know now I received divine help from above when I chose Drake Software as our partner to help us expand our tax business.

Today, Drake Software has grown into a significant company and is a tax industry leader. But behind the millions of tax returns filed each year through Drake Software, The Drake Family STILL is the company to choose when you want a tax software partner to help you take your tax business to the next level.

Chauncey Hutter, Sr.
Successful Tax Business Owner

Top 10 Reasons Why Successful Tax Pros Use DRAKE Software

www.MillionDollarTaxBiz.com/Drake

1. As you build your business, finding the right professional relationships and knowing who and what you can count on is essential. You need to find partners who understand your company's needs and deliver innovative products that improve your efficiency, productivity, and profitability. Drake Software has done that for us, from pioneering electronic filing and developing common-sense Accounting and Payroll software, to maintaining preparer-centric customer support and acquiring paperless tools and scanning and filling automation solutions.

2. Anyone who's picked up a software survey in either AICPA's Journal of Accountancy or NATP's Tax Pro Journal over the past few years will undoubtedly have seen Drake Software consistently receive top marks in areas like quality of customer service, price, and overall customer satisfaction. It's that consistent value – that drive to produce a comprehensive tax package that can serve the needs of a firm, regardless of size, at a reasonable price ... (and even help you build a million dollar tax practice.)

3. When you sit down to renew your tax software package, it's always nice to know that you're getting everything you need for one set price. Guesswork is the last thing anyone wants to deal with when getting prepared

for tax season, and Drake doesn't sell their software piecemeal. Since opening their doors in 1976, they have focused on giving tax preparers – if you'll pardon the cliché – more bang for their buck, and this is just another way they've delivered year after year. Drake makes sure their tax package includes everything preparers need to get through tax season: office management tools, accounting and payroll, paperless document management, and solid conversion software. When considering both the price tag and the services delivered, you can't find a better value in tax prep software. And that's not even counting their customer service, which is at a level unheard of in today's world. They actually answer the telephone with a real support person, during the peak of tax season, in seconds, not minutes (or hours…YIKES!)

4. Unfortunately, preparing taxes sometimes means making a call to customer support during the peak of filing season; we've all been there. That's why it's reassuring to know that you'll only ever wait a few seconds before getting ahold of somebody on the phone. But if you don't want to call someone, you can always access one of Drake's online tutorial videos. That's one of the best things about Drake: they're proactive when it comes to providing information, training, CPE opportunities, and, generally speaking, keeping you up to date on changes in the industry.

5. Good accounting and payroll software can make your life much easier, especially as your practice expands. Drake's Client Write-Up program easily handles single- and multiple-office accounting issues. Aside from handling bookkeeping and payroll, it provides detailed

financial reports, includes tax and wage forms, and can even help you set up direct deposits and Web-based payroll. If your practice doesn't tackle accounting services, you can still use CWU to make e-file versions of IRS forms, like W-2s or 1099s.

6. While e-filing is not a new development in 2015, it was in 1986 when Drake pioneered the way we would submit tax returns almost 30 years later. Drake has always had their eye on using software to improve the efficiency of preparing tax returns, so it comes as no surprise when quality of life improvements like integrating e-signature pads to better streamline e-filing pop up, alongside diagnostic and source document management improvements.

7. Online information security has been a hot topic following recent high-profile data breaches, like the hack of the IRS's "Get Transcript" program. The online world is not new to Drake, and they have always put data security at the top of their priorities. Drake's on-line portals (SecureFilePro) allows secure delivery of documents to and from your clients, giving them peace of mind and showing your firm's commitment to using the right technology to keep your clients' sensitive information secure.

8. Implementing technology can be a huge investment and time consuming. The sheer scope of maintaining software updates, ensuring software is compatible with operating systems, dealing with hard drive crashes and all of the other things that go along with technology can be overwhelming. One intriguing idea is to consider outsourcing at least part of that process by utilizing hosted products such as Drake Hosted. It allows

everyone in the firm to access the same server from any computer with internet access securely. Drake maintains the server on their platform and keeps everything up to date and running smoothly. All you have to do is login and work. Perfect!

9. Much has been said about converting to a paperless tax office to improve client document organization, and there are great tools available to help preparers take advantage of the time- and space-saving benefits of making the switch. Since the Drake Document Manager automatically stores return document PDFs in customizable client folders, you'll spend even less time manually organizing client files in the software. And that's a far cry from having to fetch a printout and take it to the metal filing cabinet.

10. GruntWorx, Drake's web-based tax automation company, improves on client document management by automatically organizing scanned client documents. On those busy days when you have to scan dozens of clients' documents, it can be tedious to have to arrange them in the proper order before feeding them through the scanner. Luckily, the Organizer doesn't require any presorting; you just scan the documents and send them to GruntWorx and you'll get back a bookmarked, searchable, and organized PDF. Well worth a few dollars per return.

Bonus (Reason #11)

11. Drake's Populate service takes the whole process a step further by pulling the client data from those scanned source files to insert it into the appropriate fields on tax forms. Everything from W-2s to huge brokerage

statements can be sent through the Gruntworx system, which means you are not keying information by hand. This cuts prep time substantially, allowing you to spend time reviewing the final product and talking with clients about expanding your services or gaining referrals, which means you are growing your business. Smart.

www.DrakeSoftware.com

Healthcare Tax Pro Success

The ACA Expert Authority Fast-Track System

Makes You The Automatic Go-To
Tax Professional In Your City

www.MillionDollarTaxBiz.com/ACAExpert

Your Own Book ... Already DONE-FOR-YOU!

THE Ultimate Turn-Key ACA Expert
Positioning Selling Tool

www.MillionDollarTaxBiz.com/ACABook

Blair Whitworth

Like most tax professionals I had no idea when the Affordable Care Act was passed, that it would have ANY impact on the tax industry. In 2010 (when Obamacare was signed into law) I was the president of a multi-location tax preparation chain with 35 offices and thousands of clients. While I realized that healthcare would change because of the ACA, my attention was focused on growing our brand and dealing with the challenges of a competitive marketplace.

However, in 2012, I began serving on the IRS Electronic Tax Administration Advisory Committee (ETAAC). One of the first presentations I heard was on the IRS implementation of the ACA, and the challenges the agency faced in managing all the administrative components of the legislation. I was completely floored. Like most people I thought of the Affordable Care Act as just concerning healthcare. I had no idea there was any substantive relationship with taxation.

That series of meetings in 2012 changed my vantage point on the future of our tax preparation offices, and on the industry as a whole. It was clear that, whether I liked it or not, healthcare and taxation were soon to be intertwined, with huge implications for the future.

While I was busy leading our multi-location company, I was also helping other tax professionals in growing and developing their businesses. After learning about the impact of the ACA I immediately knew: (a) I had to figure-out how to handle the strategic and operational implications for our chain; and (b) I needed to share this information with my colleagues and partners in the tax industry.

During the next couple of years I developed programs for how to integrate ACA services into our retail tax prep operational structure. I concentrated on tools that would allow us to achieve the benefits of the ACA, and minimize the "pain" or headache of all these new rules and regulations. Of course, the Affordable Care Act has been rolling-out in phases, so it's a constant practice of facing new challenges, and the best way to respond.

In 2014 we sold our retail tax preparation chain to a major competitor. That left me able to focus my attention on providing ACA consulting services to independent tax business owners.

Can you name the two subjects
that are the most distasteful
and confusing to the average
consumer?

I bet the vast majority of people would include **healthcare** and **taxation** at the very top of the list.

Both are:

- Governed by arcane rules that change frequently and truly are understood by almost nobody

- Overseen by multiple bureaucratic federal and state agencies

- Two of the largest household expenses in the budget

The passage of the Affordable Care Act has merged these two arenas into one: double the headache and double the confusion. Healthcare is now intricately linked to the tax code. And who will have to sort-through all this confusion? The answer is the tax professional community. The problem is that most preparers know little or nothing about healthcare. But it's no longer a choice.

Health-Care Tax-Pro Success is a consulting service that provides resources for the tax-professional community on how to effectively implement the ACA in their practice. We provide tools in education, training, operations, compliance, and marketing. All are designed to enable the tax business owner to profit from this new world of taxes and healthcare and at the same limit the headaches of all these new rules.

TaxProMarketer

The Online Marketing Earthquake:

How Your Tax or Accounting Firm Can Profit THIS Tax Season

www.MillionDollarTaxBiz.com/OnlineMarketing

Nate Hagerty

... is *the* Tax Pro Marketer and has **a proven, straight-forward approach that combines the tried and true staples of successful marketing with cutting edge digital tactics.**

Knowing the audience is the key to any marketing effort, and Nate has his finger on the pulse of the professional service shopper. Early on, the potential client, especially in the tax industry, is typically in information-gathering mode. During this time, a conversational tone goes a long way and stands out from the normal herd of block text and stoicism found in other professional service marketing.

TaxProMarketer is the foremost marketing firm for small- to mid-sized independent tax firms in the nation. What makes them unique (apart from the excellence of everything they do) is the relationship-orientation of their work on behalf of tax firms, combined with a deep knowledge of direct-response marketing principles.

Nate's company helps firms build deeper and stronger relationships with clients and prospects through social media, email marketing and other online channels (including their main firm website) — all so your firm can rise above the noise online and offline and build a top-of-consciousness relationship with businesses and taxpayers so they refer more, stay longer and pay you more.

For the complete online tax business marketing experience (everything done-for-you), Nate's team delivers an internet promotional system in a full suite. Your tax professional website is hand-built and custom-made on the WordPress platform. It offers all of the slickness and features which today's web surfers are used to, but again – carrying a refreshing tone and approach. Complete with video and a custom-tailored look, the site provides a venue for tax and accounting professionals to build authority, while still maintaining accessibility. Autoresponders immediately follow up with site visitors.

If you're ready to take your tax firm to the next level, Nate Hagerty is someone with a proven record of helping grow million-dollar tax businesses.

ATOM
Automated Tax Office Manager

How to Easily & Efficiently Organize Your Tax Office Saving Time & Money ... Guaranteed!

www.MillionDollarTaxBiz.com/ATOM

Mark Pricco

In 1990, I graduated from Michigan State University with a bachelor degree in Accounting. I then accepted an auditing position with the Department of Defense Inspector General Office in Washington DC. I got my CPA in 1994 and started preparing tax returns part-time with Jackson Hewitt. In 1997, my dad was diagnosed with lung cancer, so I moved back home to Lansing, MI to be closer to my family and to begin working with my dad in his insurance agency (Pohl Insurance Agency, Inc.). In addition to selling insurance I started my tax business out of the same office. In 1998, X-TAX was established and I prepared 75 returns in my first year of business.

In 1999, I received Chauncey's marketing material in the mail. I was eager to grow my business, and this seemed to be the answer. I read everything and asked for more. I couldn't get enough. I wanted to run my office just like his. I believe I attended my first boot camp in the fall of 1999. I implemented as many of his marketing ideas as I could that first year. I used his direct mail, refer-a-friend program, TV ads, etc. All I did is replaced his company name with my company name and it worked. The results were unbelievable. My numbers tripled the first year.

- 1999 – 75 to 225 returns
- 2000 - 225 to 500 returns
- 2001 – 500 to 1250 returns
- 2002 – 1250 to 2600 returns

The marketing was working great but my office was in chaos. There was no organization: file folders were being lost, tracking client status was difficult, we were unable to track marketing methods, and staff morale was awful. We were working long days and nights. As my dad put it, I was "flying by the seat of my pants." But I didn't want to stop the marketing because it was unbelievable how easy it was to get people in the door. It was my job to figure a way to bring order to the office.

In 2002, I again attended Chauncey's annual boot camp, but this time I was looking for help in organization. I knew the marketing worked, but I wanted to improve the flow of the office. I asked other attendees what they were doing and it became obvious that nobody really had a good method of organizing their offices. Everyone just worked long hours and gave up family time during tax season. At the boot camp, I adopted many of the organization techniques Chauncey's offices were using at the time, but I wanted to do more for my office. I thought the answer to my office problems was to automate as many job functions as possible. I looked for an office management tool in the current market, but I couldn't find anything, so in the fall of 2003 I decided to build it myself. With help from my brother-in-law, we built our first software package in Microsoft Access that tracked marketing, cash receipts and client notes, and we put it to the test in the 2003 filing season (Jan 2004).

X-TAX continued to grow, bringing on more clients and more employees, and the software package as is, was NOT doing the job I wanted it to do. It helped, but it was not doing enough for the office. So in the fall of 2005, I hired a professional software developer to make the needed improvements to the software. In the summer of 2007, we started marketing ATOM to other tax business owners around the country.

Today I am still using Chauncey's marketing materials and this past year we prepared over 8,000 tax returns with 3 offices and 46 employees. Unlike those early years, my office is now under control, and I know where everything is and I know my numbers. With ATOM I have automated almost everything in our office, and in doing so I go home right after we close our doors even on our busiest days.

The IRS Resolution Business

Michael Rozbruch's Tax & Business Solutions Academy™

"6 Secrets to a 7 Figure Tax Resolution Practice"

(EVEN IF YOU ARE <u>NOT</u> A CPA OR ENROLLED AGENT)

www.MillionDollarTaxBiz.com/IRSHelpBiz

Michael Rozbruch

...went from a dead broke, and in debt (up to his eyeballs) CPA, to having built one of the largest, most successful and reputable tax resolution firms in the country. He came straight out of the corporate world, with zero IRS/Tax Resolution experience, and went on to personally represent nearly 2,000 individuals and small business owners before the IRS over a 16-year span. Most of it self-taught.

Mike says, "If I could do that, anybody can!" Today, he trains and coaches CPAs/EAs/Attorneys **and non-licensed practitioners** through his Tax & Business Solutions Academy by revealing how to add highly profitable IRS Problem Clients to their practices through proven marketing, sales, client control/practice management and case resolution strategies.

There is NO other program that exists today that provides the level of hand-held monthly implementation coaching support to its members like Mike does.

Michael is the former president of the prestigious National Association of Tax Resolution Companies and is a member of the CPE committee of ASTPS. Michael has been featured numerous times as the guest expert on the Fox News Network, KCAL and KABC. His interviews and expertise have been published in Inc. Magazine, Tax Analysts® "Tax Notes Today", U.S. News & World Report, The Wall Street Journal, and Entrepreneur Magazine, to name a few. As a Certified Tax Resolution Specialist (CTRS) and CPA, he has represented thousands of taxpayers who owe the IRS, but simply cannot afford to pay.

Michael has been a guest speaker at conferences and has been interviewed on numerous TV news programs as a nationally recognized expert guest speaker. In 2009, CPA Magazine honored Michael with the prestigious national recognition of Top Tax Advisor to Know during Recession. He was also named an Executive of the Year Finalist in the 2009 American Business Awards.

In addition, Michael accepted a Bronze Stevie Award for the "2012 Maverick of the Year" title on behalf of the American Business Awards, which recognized his work as an expert in the tax resolution industry for the past 16 years. He has been interviewed by hundreds of radio stations and has appeared numerous times as a guest expert on national TV, including

Fox News.

If you have any desire to learn how to find hidden gems, right under your nose and light a fire in your sales and profits... or simply want to learn how to jump in and get your first tax resolution case resolved with confidence, then Michael Rozbruch is your man!

ducerus
Your Total College Solution

"How To Master A Unique Market Niche To Explode Your Tax Practice, Dominate Your Competition, And Make Yourself the ONLY Financial Person Your Clients Will Ever Talk To Again, While Getting Up To Five Income Streams For Each Client ... Guaranteed!"

www.MillionDollarTaxBiz.com/ducerus

Ron Caruthers

Ducerus has eighteen offices in ten states, listed on *Inc. Magazine's* Fastest Growing Companies in 2014. Ron's been quoted in *Entrepreneur, The Wall Street Journal, USA Today* and *Inc. Magazine*. In addition, Ron is routinely featured on *FOX, ABC, NBC & CBS* and co-authored *New York Times* Bestseller, Shift Happens.

Ron Caruthers has a very exclusive position within the financial services industry, and has built a seven-figure practice of less than 200 clients a year. He is not a tax preparer, but has mastered the art of getting clients to call him first for all their financial needs, and he refers out enough tax prep work to keep two tax preparers busy year round.

More importantly, Ron has clientele that happily pay him well in excess of what a top attorney gets, follow all of his instructions to a 'T', and refer Ron and his staff to their friends and family like crazy ...

This opportunity is the next big thing in the tax preparing business right now!

You'll learn how to position yourself to get paid up to five times for every client you deal with, not just once anymore, AND how to set up a unique revenue stream that will allow you to get paid year-round and not just during tax season!

This IS the real deal.

Now, Chauncey said not to get into the specifics of what marketplace Ron works in now, but I will tell you this: There are over 5 million new prospects for Ron's service every year. And not only that, his clients pay a fee for the advice (usually around $4,000) PLUS they'll drive for hours through heavy traffic just to meet with Ron. And, that initial fee is just the start of the relationship, because most of these clients use Ron for everything from that point forward...from mortgages (Ron has a system so YOU can offer this service to your clients immediately AND get paid for it, even if you don't know anything about that business) to all of their other investments.

In fact, Ron gets paid up to five times for each client.

Ron Caruthers Will Teach You:

- How to master a unique market niche that has over 19 million existing prospects, and over 5 million new prospects each year, that allows you to charge fees year round and get paid retainers by your clients, just like an attorney, AND get added fees for the additional services they implement.

- How to make a consistent, year-round high six figure net income off a minimal amount of clients.

- How to never be 'fee-shopped' again.

- How to completely dominate your market area, so you never have to worry about newer or cheaper tax preparers, online tax software, or H&R Block again.

- How to find clients that want help way beyond what Turbo Tax could ever give them, so your fees will never be questioned again.

- How to increase your referral business by 500%.

- How to have your office booked up like a top surgeon's office with people waiting weeks to get in to see you -- year round, and not just during tax season.

- How to be viewed as a specialist and professional in your town, and no longer as a commodity that software or another firm can replace.

- How to master a unique selling angle that allows you to charge $2,000 to $6,000 a client, not $200-$300.

- How to master the concept of multiple paydays from each client.

- How to get clients to travel to you, up to four hours each way! (Ron currently has several clients who come from 1-4 hours each way to meet with him...and he will teach you how to have that happen also...again, because you'll be viewed as a specialist)

- How to build a clientele that truly appreciates what you do, and continually thanks you and wants to introduce you to their friends AND invite you to their parties.

"I've looked at hundreds of quality opportunities for tax and accounting professionals in the last two decades ... I believe what Ron Caruthers reveals in this training is one of THE best opportunities I've ever seen for tax business owners (especially right now with the tax industry is such transition) ... do NOT miss this!"

Chauncey Hutter, Jr.

Real Tax Business Success™

Get Access to OVER 101 Insider Tax Business Success Tools and other Money-Making Tax Office Profit Strategies Pivotal in Building Chauncey's Multi-Million Dollar Tax Business!

www.taxmarketing.com/MillionDollarTaxBiz

Made in the USA
Charleston, SC
03 December 2016